De-Stressing Your Life

DIANE STOUT

VICTOR BOOKS

A DIVISION OF SCRIPTURE PRESS PUBLICATIONS INC.
USA CANADA ENGLAND

Dedicated to those who have been dedicated to me:
God, who guided me.
My family (Jim, Mark, and David), who supported me.
My friends (Betty and Debbie), who encouraged me.
My editor (Carolyn), who believed in me.
My women's groups, who inspired me.

Unless otherwise noted, Scripture quotations are from the *Holy Bible, New International Version®*. Copyright © 1973, 1978, 1984 by International Bible Society. Used by permission of Zondervan Publishing House. All rights reserved. Other quotations are from *The Amplified Bible* (AMP) © 1954, 1958 The Lockman Foundation.

Editor: Carolyn Nystrom
Designer: Grace K. Chan Mallette
Cover Photo: William Koechling

Recommended Dewey Decimal Classification: 248.4
Suggested Subject Heading: PERSONAL RELIGION: CONDUCT OF CHRISTIAN LIFE
ISBN: 1-56476-325-0

1   2   3   4   5   6   7   8   9   10   Printing/Year   99   98   97   96   95

VICTOR BOOKS
A division of SP Publications, Inc.
1825 College Avenue, Wheaton, Illinois 60187

CONTENTS

INTRODUCTION

Living with stress is like being a piece of elastic. Stretched. Expected to spring back.

Tough. Tested everyday. To function effectively in today's society, women must be resilient, rapidly recovering from stressful demands. We will never be free of stress, so we must learn to cope with it. God gives us a way to bounce back with renewed strength. By practicing God's advice, women can begin to take active steps in dealing with pressures. The stronger we are on the inside, the better we can cope with difficulties on the outside.

Knowledge won't change the quality of our lives unless we use it. *De-Stressing Your Life* offers practical ways to live God's truth on a daily basis. Even if we can't reach perfection, we make the concept "ours" when we see even a small amount of success with the change.

Change is difficult, but not impossible. God's ways are not our ways, but if we dare to let Him work in our daily lives, He teaches us. To *act* differently, we must *think* differently. By relying on God's principles, we can begin to de-stress by learning to release tension, to deal with emotions, to form healthy attitudes, and to accept ourselves and others.

This book is designed for a discussion group and/or individual study. Women will have opportunities to grow by spending time with God, self, and others. The study includes the following sections:

- **From Stress to Source.** Each chapter will begin with our best source of knowledge: the Bible.
- **From Stress to Strength.** The study will continue with a narrative section giving stories of personal application.
- **From Stress to Action.** An idea is not "ours" until we use it. Putting what we study into practice is the heartbeat of this book.

This section offers activities that help us take ownership of God's truth on a daily basis.

❦ **Group Guide.** Women learn from other women. As the group follows the discussion questions, they will be led to think, to share, to do. The group studies (including one for an introductory meeting) are found in the back of the book. Since the emphasis of this book is practice, the group studies help women to share stories of God's work in their lives.

A vital part of stimulating personal growth is a *Spiritual Notebook.* Use it for the activities in *From Stress to Action.* But this study can only begin targeting specific spiritual lessons. By using a three-ringed binder, you can continue to add new ideas of your own.

As you study this book . . .

> may you develop a closer relationship with God.
> may you discover that your Source of strength is always with you.
> may you come to know Him as your best friend.

—DS

TAKE IT, GOD
De-Stress by Praying

Philippians 4:4-13

FROM STRESS TO SOURCE

Barbara fell across her bed, sobbing into the pillow. "I can't take it anymore. Everything is caving in on me. The pressure is too much. I'm going to burst. I'm pulled so many different directions that I don't know which way to turn. No matter how hard I try, I can't get a handle on my life. I'm stressed out."

1. Read Philippians 4:4-13. Barbara is a Christian woman living under stress. Name several prescriptions found in the passage that will help give her inner peace.

2. What do these verses tell you about God? (Search the entire passage.)

3. If you were Barbara's friend, what would you say to her if she tried to practice Philippians 4:4-7, but she still didn't feel peaceful?

4. The *NIV Study Bible* footnote for verse 6 states that thanksgiving is "the antidote to worry." Think of a time when your prayers didn't *seem* like they were answered. In looking back at that situation, what could you thank God for now?

5. Reread verses 8 and 9. What would you think about if you practiced these verses?

6. Choose one way to implement verses 8-9 this week. For additional ideas, refer to *From Stress to Action*, activities 2 and 3.

7. Think of the last time you felt stressed. Check phrases that describe how you handled the situation.

denied it	worried	talked to a pro-
prayed	analyzed it	fessional counselor
talked to spouse	exercised	threw things
talked to friend	talked to pastor	shopped
became irritable	lashed out at others	read a book
accepted it	handled it	cried it out
avoided it	became ill	laughed it off
bottled it inside	read Scripture	other _____
rested	ate	

8. Circle phrases from the list above that show constructive ways of handling stress. Compare checked and circled phrases. Are you practicing what you know is best? Which ones could help your situation?

9. Do you generally turn to God when the problem first arises, when it reaches crisis level, or when it's over and you're reflecting on what you should have done? Why?

10. What obstacles keep you from releasing your stress to God?

11. How can you overcome these obstacles? (Follow up with *From Stress to Action*, activity 1.)

12. In Philippians 4:10-11, Paul thanks the Philippians for their financial support of his ministry, but he indicates that he has learned to be content with or without finances. In view of verse 12, what steps do you think he took in his life to learn this secret?

13. Explain how discontent with financial status can produce stress—whether the individual is rich or poor.

14. On a scale of 1–10, what is your level of contentment?

Overall?   Personally?
Financially?   Spiritually?

15. By practicing his own advice, Paul could affirm Philippians 4:13. If you were as bold as Paul, what differences could you see in your daily life?

16. What is adding stress to your life right now? Which things can you release and which ones are hard for you to let go?

17. If you have experienced God's peace during a stressful situation, describe how you felt before and after you prayed.

Even if you have never experienced this peace, release a specific stress at this time by following this procedure. Use your *Spiritual Notebook* to:

🐾 Praise God for who He is by writing or saying His qualities.

🐾 Write or say one specific stress point that you are ready to release. Tell Him *exactly* how you feel about it.

🐾 Ask God to give you wisdom, understanding, acceptance, or guidance in this area as you turn the stress over to Him.

🐾 Thank Him for how He is already working in the situation. Expect good things from Him and accept what He gives.

🐾 Later, if the pressure about the specific item comes back, continue to thank Him for taking care of things even if you can't see the answer yet.

FROM STRESS TO STRENGTH

Darkness engulfed the room. Time for action. Herman darted through the small opening, itching to be on the run. He pushed as hard as he could on the slippery surface, gaining momentum with each lunge. His pace quickened and now he ran at top speed. Herman was really moving, but where was he going? Nowhere. He was only spinning his wheel in his gerbil cage.

When I'm stressed out, my mind is like Herman going round and round. Running, but going nowhere. As the pressures of the day build, my inner peace turns to turmoil as my mind races on the gerbil wheel. *When will Mark get a job? . . . I need to do the laundry. . . . Should we put Grandma in a nursing home? . . . I need to work late so I can catch up. . . . The school meeting is the same time as David's baseball game. . . .* My mind dashes from one demand to another, spinning the unrest into a tangled web of emotions. When I'm stressed out, I waste mental energy by spinning my wheels like Herman. But God didn't intend for me to be a gerbil. He gave me the choice to get off my wheel and do something—pray.

Praying (God's prescription for relieving stress) is simple to say but hard to practice. Praying on a daily basis becomes a battle between self-discipline and busy schedules. Yet, it is my strength.

Praying is like following the doctor's orders. My doctor prescribes medicine for me, but unless I fill the prescription and swallow the pill, I won't get well. I don't like taking medicine, but I do it because it will help me in the long-run. Consistent praying is difficult, but it strengthens my inner being so I can cope better with anxieties. Just as the doctor looks at my physical body from the "outside-in," God looks at my spiritual body from the "inside-out."

Christian women aren't immune to stress, but they have an inside track for coping with it. *The Amplified Version* of Philippians 4:6 explains, "Do not fret or have any anxiety about anything, but in every circumstance . . . continue to make your wants known to God."

Praying about every stress is a big pill to swallow—yet, it is God's prescription. If I can't take all the medicine in one gulp, I could cut the pill in half and swallow what I can. (Sometimes half a dose is better than no medicine at all.) I may not be able to release every anxiety when it occurs, but at least I can begin to release some of my concerns. God will meet me at my level of understanding and gradually take me into a deeper relationship until I can experience more. I

11

can't outgive God. The more I release to Him, the more inner peace I experience. Laying my concerns at His feet is the prescription. God's peace is the evidence that the medicine is working.

In addition to the prayer prescription, God helps us cope with stress by using people. People who support. People who laugh. People who hear. People with hearts. People with big shoulders. People with tears. People who care. We need people, whether they are a spouse, friend, or coworker.

Friends are crucial, but sometimes we need professional guidance to learn skills in dealing with relationships and pressures. God is the Healer. But just as God often heals our bodies by using doctors, He (the Master Counselor) often heals our inner beings by working *through* professionals. Seeking professional help is a sign of strength, showing that we are serious about dealing with our problems rather than spinning on the gerbil wheel.

Whether we confide in family, friends, pastor, social worker, psychologist, or psychiatrist, we all need a release valve. Expressing inner struggles puts the problems out in the open so we can see them clearly. Then we can begin to manage our stress.

As the world becomes more complex, relationships and responsibilities become more entangled. Unless we live in "la-la land," we all have suffered from stress at one time or another. We'll never be stress-free, but we can diminish it by learning to manage it. We must control stress or it will control us.

The first step in dealing with stress is the hardest: deciding to do something about it. Decision holds power. Deciding to release the steam valve as the pressure builds enables us to begin to experience God's peace. Realizing that we can't completely rid ourselves of pressure, we *can* take active steps to relieve inner turmoil while dealing with outward circumstances.

Dealing with pressure is like flying an airplane. When there is no turbulence, the plane flies on automatic. But as the storm brews, the pilot takes over the controls and guides the plane manually.

During calm weather my flight is smooth and I'm happy. But when stress comes, I lose my inner peace. Left on automatic, my plane shakes as it hurls through the air, tossed by demands on my time, energy, and emotions. When I *decide* to do something about my plight, I take action. Does this mean I take the steering column and fly the plane myself? No. I give it to the real Pilot. The One who knows the course without using the automatic instruments. The One who knows how to get through the storm. Jesus.

Deciding to pray and put Jesus in the pilot's seat is my first course of action. Letting Jesus direct my course, I can fly through the storm with confidence that He is in charge. Though I must go *through* the storm, I trust the pilot to maneuver the plane in the rough spots and bring me to safety. I can't see the way. I'm scared. I don't know what will happen. But I trust my Pilot.

Does "praying out" our tension sound too simple to be realistic? Contrary to what many people understand, turning to God is not a passive cop-out for facing a problem. Aggressive faith is taking action and requires energy to keep our minds in line with our beliefs. Hannah Whitall Smith, in her classic book *The Christian's Secret of a Happy Life*, emphasizes that God's job is to work and our job is to trust. Praying is giving the problem up to God—not giving up on the problem. Christians have been ridiculed for having "blind faith," but the term is a misnomer. Faith is having our eyes open and clearly fixed on the One in Whom we trust.

Even Jesus was pressured as He ministered to people's physical and spiritual needs. Crowds demanded His time, men plotted to kill Him, and His followers didn't understand Him. Jesus knew what stress was, but He released it by going regularly to His Father in prayer. (Luke 5:15-16; 6:11-12; Matthew 14:22-23).

It is essential that we connect to God's renewing strength in the same way Jesus did. As we experiment with different methods of prayer, each of us must find what best links us to our Heavenly Father. The important thing is to find an avenue that works for us on a regular basis.

My prayer life takes wings in a spiral notebook. Writing my prayers every day gives me a constant vehicle for reducing stress. Whether I'm angry, sad, exuberant, concerned, or "stressed out," writing my feelings releases tension out of my system and up to God. I identify what is bothering me when I quit rambling in my mind and put it on paper. Then I can leave it. Praying specifically enables me to present my requests to God. As I transfer my anxieties to paper, I release emotional baggage and put my situation in His hands. God is "in" the problem.

When I am spiritually low, my faith is revitalized as I look at past prayers in my notebook. I see His answers. Some are "yes." Some are "no." Some are "not yet, Diane." I don't know how He will answer, but I know His *hand* is in my problems when I seek His *face* in my prayers.

Although most women who write their prayers find it therapeutic, journaling is not the only avenue to God. Experimenting with different methods keeps our prayer life vital. Pray out loud. Repeat Scripture back to God. Pray while kneeling, walking, or enjoying a sunset. Sing or listen to praise music. Whether we pray at a church altar or alone in a car, the important thing is that we do it on a regular basis. Prayer is our lifeline to God.

Consistent praying is like keeping our gas tanks filled so we aren't stranded on a highway with an empty tank. When the gas gauge is low, the warning light signals us to take care of the problem. If we don't refill our spiritual fuel tanks with God's resources, we can't expect to travel far on His road. Filling the car one time isn't enough. We need to replenish our spiritual energy by praying every day so a crisis won't catch us on empty.

Sometimes I pray, but my spiritual gas tank doesn't seem to "fill up." I try to release my teenage son to Him, but when I can't see any results I become discouraged. When I'm empty, I think that God isn't working. Hebrews 11:1 says, "Now faith is being sure of what we hope for and certain of what we do not see." I can't see an answer for my son, but I can be certain that God is *in* the situation. My hope lies in the One who gives the answer, not in what the answer is. The more I know *who* God is, the more hope I have. This hope allows me to wait, to believe, to thank.

In the past, I didn't pray until things got bad enough for God to take over. I let tension mount with my husband before I prayed. School and church activities overwhelmed me before I prayed. My faith was a spiritual roller coaster, peaking and nose-diving, slamming me into unexpected turns of life. After years of crisis praying, I finally began to follow God's prescription for inner peace by going straight to my knees at the *first* sign of conflict. Forming the habit of quickly turning problems over to Him has become my primary way to diminish stress. I still shortchange myself when I don't practice what I know, but now it doesn't take long for me to realize what I need to do: pray.

Before I learned this principle, dealing with stress felt like I was in a swimming pool trying to keep three beach balls underwater at the same time. I could hold one down, but when I tried to control the others, the first one popped up. It was an exhausting, never-ending battle. Pushing. Fighting. Failing.

Prayer wraps God's "net" around the beach balls so they are more manageable. When His presence surrounds the things that stress me out, the beach balls may still surface, but I can cope with them better if they're contained in a net. I have a way of dealing with them because they are wrapped in prayer. After covering the beach balls with the net, I tie them to an anchor which holds them underwater. I handle my stress better with the net of prayer covering my anxieties because I know who the Anchor is—God.

FROM STRESS TO ACTION

Use your *Spiritual Notebook* to:

🐛 Establish a regular "quiet time." If praying every day overwhelms you, start by praying three times a week. Date your prayers and notice the difference in your days when you pray.

🐛 Occupy your mind with God's qualities by reading the Bible and Christian books, listening to Christian music or teaching tapes, joining a Christian discussion group, or telling a friend or your spouse how God is working in your life. Which method will you practice this week?

🐛 Replace doubts, worry, and distress by reading and reflecting on one or more of the following passages. Genesis 1; Psalm 23, 34, 100, 103, 104, 145, 146, 147, 150; Isaiah 40, 42:1-17; Johr 17; 1 Corinthians 13. Which one speaks to you?

🐛 If you are angry at God for *not* answering your prayer as you expected, write a complaint letter to Him in your *Spiritual Notebook*. Read it aloud and visualize God listening intently. Sit quietly and allow time for God to respond to you and meet you in your anger.

2

IT'S ABOUT TIME
De-Stress by
Setting Priorities

Matthew 6:25-34

From Stress to Source

You sit in the doctor's office, numb with disbelief, yet somehow relieved that the words are finally said. The words. The words you dreaded to hear pound over and over in your head, each time cutting deeper, stinging with the harsh reality of death. "You have six months to live—maybe a year."

The doctor's pat on your shoulder jars you out of your stupor. Slowly, he leads you from his office to face the world—a world that looks totally different to you now. You must get control of yourself, get your affairs in order, and . . . then what?

How will you spend the last days of your life? What is really important to you? Walking out of the doctor's office, trying to hold your head high, you take a deep breath and resolve not to waste your time while you have it.

1. Read Matthew 6:25-34. Name at least three lessons found in the passage.

2. How would these lessons improve your quality of life?

3. According to these verses, why can we trust God to take care of our needs?

4. Matthew 6:27 shows the futility of worry. Name several reasons we still do it.

5. In verse 33, Jesus states what our first priority should be. Write a paragraph describing what seeking His kingdom and His righteousness means to you.

6. When we are "right" with God, His Spirit fills our inner beings. Certain qualities (fruit of the Spirit) naturally result from this inner righteousness. Record these qualities found in Galatians 5:22.

7. Which fruit would you like to see ripen in your life? Why?

8. If our first priority in life were to seek God, how could it *reduce* our stress level?

9. How could it *increase* our stress level?

10. If you had six months to live, what changes would you make in your daily schedule?

11. Read thoughtfully Matthew 6:34. What are the benefits of following these instructions?

12. Check the areas you think about the most.

finances	social activities	friends
children	career	personal goals
recreation	husband	future
education	spiritual growth	past
church functions	hobbies	present
household	God	other _____

13. From the list above, circle areas that produce stress. Which things can you change? Which must you accept? If you have trouble accepting a certain problem, go through the steps for releasing a specific stress as outlined under question 17 on page 10. Ask God to help you.

14. Psalm 37:4 says, "Delight yourself in the LORD and He will give you the desires of your heart." List several personal goals that you never have time to do.

15. Which areas listed in question 12 prevent you from pursuing your desires? Why?

16. To get a better idea of how you spend your time, track your day by writing down in your *Spiritual Notebook* what you do every hour. Try to record at least three full days. Highlight different areas with different colors. (A different color for household, career, travel, family, self, spiritual, entertainment, other.) Analyze which ones are fixed and which could be changed. Write a brief summary here, then bring your full record to the group session for the follow-up activity.

17. List your priorities in your *Spiritual Notebook*. Take your time in doing this evaluation. Compare your priorities with your daily schedule. Be honest with yourself. Are you putting your time on what's important to you? Extend this exercise with *From Stress to Action*, activity 1.

FROM STRESS TO STRENGTH

The two women sat at the kitchen table sipping coffee, engrossed in deep conversation. Jenny sat on the edge of her chair, hanging on every word of her older companion. She had admired Martha for three years. Sharing tears of joy and pain had bonded the two women like mother and daughter.

"Martha, being your neighbor is the best thing that has happened to me," Jenny said. "You seem to stay at peace with yourself, no matter what happens. How do you do it?"

"Walnuts and beans."

"What? I don't get it," Jenny said.

Martha went to her kitchen window, brought back a jar, and emptied it in front of Jenny. Walnuts and pinto beans scattered across the table.

"When I was your age, I started my day with beans." As Martha talked, she put one bean at a time back into the jar. "I began the day with a load of laundry. Then I might pay the bills, call the dentist, take the kids to school, and on and on until all my beans were in the jar.

"Falling in bed, exhausted by the day's activities, I'd remember the walnuts, the things that really mattered to me." Martha tried to fit the walnuts in the jar on top of the beans. "I hadn't made time for God; I had hardly spoken to my husband; and I had rushed my two kids through their paces without even a kind word. When I tried to shove my priorities into my schedule at the end of the day, I was too tired to pray and I couldn't spend time with my family because they were all in bed." Martha tried to put the lid on the jar, but the walnuts didn't fit.

"Then one day I decided to start with the walnuts." Martha emptied the jar once again, but this time she filled it with the walnuts first. "I got up early so I could have time with God." She put one walnut in the empty jar. "Then I took a walk with my husband and we actually talked without being interrupted by the kids." Martha added another walnut. "I hid surprise notes in my kids' lunch boxes and even tried a new hairdo before going to my meeting." Martha placed all five walnuts into the jar. "I still did my 'bean' jobs throughout the day, but they all seemed to fit around the walnuts." Martha added the rest of the beans and easily screwed the lid on the jar.

Looking intently into Jenny's eyes, Martha said, "So I try to start each day with the big things in life—walnuts."

Beans—little in size, but mighty in number. Beans are the daily "stuff" we find ourselves doing, cheating us of precious time for *being*. We all have beans, and some women have more than their fair share. But the more beans we have, the more we need to start our days with walnuts. Our best resource for handling beans is the first walnut: God.

Circumstances dictate how we spend the majority of hours, often filling our days with rigid schedules for survival. We live in a tough world that demands tough choices. If a woman is the sole provider for her family, she might be forced to work two jobs in order to make ends meet. We do what we have to do.

God gave each of us different circumstances and abilities, but He gave one thing equally to all: twenty-four hours a day. Yet we still say: "Linda has more time than I do. . . . I could spend time on myself if I had one more hour in each day. . . . I wish I had time to pray."

Rationalizing that we don't have time to do the things we want leaves us tired, discouraged, and defeated. As we stretch ourselves between careers, husbands, kids, friends, household work, recreation, physical fitness, and spiritual needs, the gift of time easily escapes our control.

The first time I put my priorities on paper, I was amazed that what I valued most was the easiest to neglect. Relationships with God, husband, and children were my high priorities, but they didn't grab my attention as fast as the shrill ring of the telephone. When I put my heart into my career, there wasn't much left when I went home. Unfortunately, I gave my best time and energy to activities that were low on my list.

Jesus clearly stated what my first priority should be: "Seek first the kingdom of God and His righteousness" (Matthew 6:33). I needed to spend time with Him, learn who I was in His eyes, and see how I fit into His family. Seeking His righteousness meant giving Him full reign to work in my daily life. This all took time.

Knowing if I didn't schedule a regular time for Him that I would never develop a close relationship, I set aside the first hour of each day for prayer.

By putting first things first, I was more open to God's guidance throughout the day because I had already "tuned in" to His presence. Now I'm hooked on God, and I can't function without my "God time." Of course I'm not perfect in keeping this schedule, but by establishing a consistent pattern and striving to keep it, I pray a lot more than I used to.

By establishing my priorities, I realized that being under the same roof with my family didn't necessarily mean I developed ties with them. My husband, Jim, isn't a demanding person, and therefore he suffered from my neglect. Due to Jim's personality, I needed to be more conscious of *making* time for him so that our relationship didn't suffer. I didn't have to worry about neglecting my children, however. They demanded my attention! Nurturing relationships requires flexibility with different types of personalities, whether it is with family or close friends.

Listing my priorities got tougher as I went down the list. My hardest decision was where to place myself. Torn between church activities, school functions, time with friends, and personal goals, I needed a crash course in time management to do everything I wanted to do.

I don't pretend to know all the answers to time management, but due to my stress level (and perhaps out of desperation), I have developed a few tricks that have helped me cope with this problem. These ideas are only sparks to kindle additional thoughts that can be adapted to different people.

Identify your working style. Do you work better by breaking a task down into small proportions, doing a little each day? Or are you project oriented and work in large blocks of time? If we understand our frameworks, we can schedule our time better and convert dead time into valuable moments for priorities.

Some people work on a project a little at a time, steadily making progress and handling goals in small doses. Women of this type keep orderly desks. A monitor could check them any day of the week and find business in order. These women clean house one hour daily. They wash a few loads of laundry each day, ironing as the clothes come out of the dryer. They diet by losing one pound a month. (They usually keep it off too.) They are methodical and work well with daily routine. They already know how to manage time, but sometimes they get "caught up" in the routine. They may need to re-focus their skills on priorities. Personalities such as these could schedule regular, short times for God, family, and self just as they organize their work.

Other people concentrate on one task until it's completely finished, no matter how long it takes. These individuals are project oriented and handle big undertakings in large chunks. Women of this type like the challenge of the big contract, the sales campaign, or generating new ideas. These women clean their entire houses on one day and don't touch the broom the rest of the week. They buy their entire wardrobe at the first of the season and plan menus by the month. They may have difficulty managing their time because they get "caught up" in what they are doing and don't allow extra time between projects. By becoming aware of their working style, these personalities could block off periods of time for priorities like they would for their projects.

Both working styles need to learn to be flexible, or they will miss magic moments with God and their families. Everybody needs a David. David is my younger son who pulls me outside to watch the meteor shower, shoves a Frisbee in my hand, or plops me down in front of a new game.

Combine activities. Bringing God into daily life adds a new dimension to daily tasks. Ironing actually becomes meaningful if I pray for the family member whose clothes I'm ironing. Waiting in the car or in the doctor's office becomes a time for spiritual growth if I have a devotional book or Bible with me. Listening to teaching or praise tapes makes driving to work (or exercising) less of a burden.

Working and playing with the family gives time for priorities and accomplishes necessary tasks. What can you do with your family? Just what you normally would do. Cook dinner, shop, paint a room, play tennis, start a craft. Schedule a family reading night. (The kids think you are spending time with them, and you're really reading the book you're dying to finish.)

Focus on one task at a time. Distractions sidetrack my purpose and become a key way of producing stress. I'm calm when I see progress, but when I "spin my wheels," it's time to focus.

Setting aside a specific time to clean house helps me focus on the task at hand. Overwhelmed by the entire house, I concentrate on one room (even one corner) before tackling another one. Cringing at the rest of the house, I feel success with my little corner—if nothing else. Focus is my by-word for time management and reducing stress. If you have a highly demanding job, being pulled in several directions at once can produce stress. Quit shuffling papers and focus on completing one task. This gives you a sense of control over demands that are otherwise unmanageable.

Take time-out for yourself. You can't be your best when you're at your worst. If I'm not careful, my R and R (rest and recreation) time becomes W and W (work and worry) time. Time-outs are as important for myself as they are for a basketball team. When the pace of the game is too fast and the team needs to settle down and focus on what they are doing, the coach calls a time-out. This breaks the cycle and puts the game back under control. I need time-outs so I can get fresh starts. Then I'm ready to move back into the game.

Plan, but be flexible. Does this statement sound contradictory? If I don't have a plan for the day, I waste time deciding what to do. Yet if I stick to my plan too tightly, I miss spontaneous events that sparkle my life.

If a friend says, "Let's have lunch sometime," she doesn't mean it if she doesn't get out her calendar. I may have good intentions of spending time with God or my family, but nothing happens if I don't schedule it. When I was trying to form the habit of a daily quiet time, I literally made appointments with God on my calendar. This sounds elementary, but it held me accountable—if only to myself.

Even though making plans is important, sometimes God has a

different agenda for me. The Good Samaritan didn't plan on his day being interrupted by a cry for help. If I'm glued to a schedule, I can't serve God when a friend needs a listening ear or a child needs a hug. Being open to His leading means I must be willing to follow.

Each of us is faced with the dilemma of following plans or being flexible. Finding the balance between personal needs and the needs of others is an art that is not easily achieved. Seeking God first is the secret of finding this ratio.

I don't keep all my priorities balanced 100 percent of the time, but I know *how* to get back on track. When things aren't going well, usually my problem is a lack of "God time." Focusing on my first priority (God) puts other concerns in perspective so I can deal with them with peace instead of emotional stress.

Indeed, "all these things will be given to you as well" (Matthew 6:33) becomes a reality when I first seek God's kingdom and righteousness. If I start my day with the walnuts, I also find room for the beans.

FROM STRESS TO ACTION

Use your *Spiritual Notebook* to do one or more of the following activities:

❦ Ask God to show you specific and creative ways to give quality time to the things that are important to you. Concentrate on one priority. Write a plan of action. Put it on your calendar three times in regular intervals (once a day, week, or month). Keep your appointments.

❦ Psalm 1 illustrates the difference in a person seeking God first with one who doesn't. Rewrite Psalm 1 for a woman, using modern language and examples. For example, "Blessed is the woman who does not seek advice from ungodly sources. . . ."

❦ Read Proverbs 31:10-31. List this woman's priorities.

❦ Write a letter to each member of your family. Tell them what they mean to you. (Give the letter only if you think it would be well received.) Sometimes the most important benefit of writing is to help the author clarify her own feelings.

❦ Live one hour as if it were your last one on earth.

3

PROBLEMS TO PLUSES
De-Stress by
Gaining Perspective

Romans 5:1-5

FROM STRESS TO SOURCE

How could this happen? One day I'm on a pedestal . . . the next day I'm in a pit. One day I'm a "ten"; the next day a "one." I'm dressed in riches; later, stripped to rags. I'm treated like a king; then sold as a slave. One day I'm safe, secure, and loved; the next day I'm an outcast, despised and scared. One day my life is a rainbow; the next day a tornado. How could they do it to me? I'm their own flesh and blood. I don't understand.

Joseph's scrambled thoughts may have sounded like these when his brothers sold him into slavery and reported him dead to their father. The rest of Joseph's story is a roller coaster of peaks and valleys, pedestals and pits. But he knew the principle of turning problems into opportunities and how to keep God's perspective while he encountered many years of hardship. How could he do this? Joseph knew how to practice the words in Romans 5:1-5. Paul wrote these words many years after Joseph's life; yet, Joseph personifies what Paul is saying.

1. Read Romans 5:1-5. Paul covers a lot of living in these few verses. Notice how he weaves faith, hope, and love throughout the passage. What else has God given us according to these verses?

2. Explain what each term in this Romans text means to you.

3. Using the following diagram, explain Romans 5:1-5 in your own words. Include why your position (being "right" with God) is the foundation for each step.

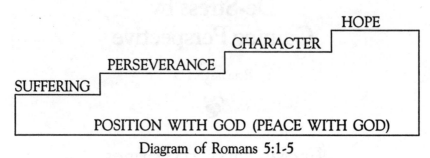

Diagram of Romans 5:1-5

4. According to Romans 5:2, our faith in Jesus Christ gives us access to His grace. Joseph's faith also gave him access to God. Using the events from his life and the *words from the diagram above,* show how Joseph lived out Romans 5:1-5. (Samples provided.) Scan Genesis 37; 39–45 for background information about Joseph.

Genesis verse	Event in Joseph's life	Concept from Romans
37:18-24	Brothers threw him in cistern.	Suffering
37:25-28		
39:1		
39:2		Position with God
39:3-4		Character
39:5		
39:8-12		

39:20		
39:21		
39:22-23		
40:14		Hope
40:23		
41:1a		
41:16,25,28		
41:33		
41:38-44		
41:50-52		
Chaps. 37; 39–45	Estranged from family 22 years	
45:7-8		
45:9-11		
45:12-15		

5. What conclusions about God's work in our lives can you draw from the previous activity?

6. Even though the Scriptures don't tell us, what do you think Joseph did to keep a good attitude through difficult times?

7. In Genesis 42–44, Joseph puts his brothers through a series of tests to prove their honesty, change of heart, and remorse over what they had done to him many years before. Do you think Joseph should have done this? Why or why not?

8. In Genesis 45:1-15, how does Joseph's attitude illustrate Romans 5:1-5?

9. If Joseph had not had God's purpose and perspective, how might he have acted toward his brothers?

   Without God's perspective in mind, what might Joseph have said to them when he revealed who he was?

10. Name several ways coping with a problem for an extended time could benefit you. Try to give specific examples. Build on this question by doing *From Stress to Action*, activity 2.

11. How can long-term problems harm you?

12. Write one lesson you could learn from the following problems.

❧ Financial problems

❧ Having an impossible boss or coworker

❧ Having a handicapped child

❧ Having a problem teenager

❧ Unemployment

❧ Health problems

❧ Problem marriage

13. A big part of dealing with problems is *accepting* them. How can this reduce stress?

14. Do you think that a person has to experience pain and problems to develop a strong character? Why or why not?

FROM STRESS TO STRENGTH

I listened intently while the women in our prayer group unfolded their problems. My heart went out to them as one crisis after another surfaced. I felt for the others, but I didn't really understand what they were experiencing. After the session was over, I told my friend, "I've had tough times, but I've never experienced a real crisis. I don't think I've been tested yet."

My friend answered, "Just wait—you will be."

She was right.

My life rocked along with a few bumps, but no real crashes. My biggest struggle (not being able to have children) seemed over when we adopted our two boys at the same time. Dad, mom, a brilliant six-year-old, and an eighteen-month bundle of joy melded together to become a family unit. We became an instant family of four. After eleven and a half years of marriage without children, my life felt like it entered a different time zone when our quiet home turned into a whirlwind of activity. The boys were a gift from God—an answered prayer—the best thing that ever happened to any of us.

Three years later, the impossible happened. I became pregnant. At age 35, this mother of two experienced her first pregnancy. I was elated, reaching a new peak of joy with what God had done.

Then it hit . . . my crisis. All of a sudden, I knew what the women in the prayer group felt. When I miscarried the baby, I went from a "ten" to a "one," from Mt. Everest to the bottom of Grand Canyon. It hurt. I didn't understand why it happened. I felt like I was thrown into a pit—like Joseph must have felt the day his brothers threw him in the cistern.

I had never experienced depression before. I found out that it was real. This time, I couldn't snap out of it just because I wanted to. I couldn't lift myself up by the boot straps. My husband was patient, but he became exasperated with me when, after three months, I still broke out into tears for no reason. I didn't know myself. I couldn't shake my feelings. I was in a crisis.

Maybe God knows how much we can take—then He brings us a breath of fresh air. Maybe time heals our pain. Maybe we learn a lesson. Maybe we don't. Maybe our faith grows. Maybe it doesn't. We don't understand why, but problems and pain are as much a part of life as happiness is.

I have gone through many dark times since my miscarriage, but I always look back to this first major crisis and try to remember what I learned. Tunnels are scary, but sometimes they're the only way to get to the other side of the mountain. Here's what I learned in my first tunnel:

—*Even if you can't see anything, keep your eyes open.*
—*Look for the light at the end of the tunnel (and hope it's not a freight train).*
—*Reach out and touch the wall—let it guide you through.*
—*Don't turn around or you'll lose your sense of direction.*
—*Step high so you don't trip over something.*
—*If someone is with you, hold his hand.*
—*Even if it's slow, keep moving.*
—*It's OK to be scared.*

During my miscarriage crisis, I walked in a tunnel. While I was still in the dark, I opened my eyes and saw something good happen. My husband and I bonded like glue. More than ever, I cherished my boys. I couldn't see God, but I reached out and clung to the wall, knowing He would eventually lead me out. My other hand grasped my family and friends as I crept through the tunnel at a snail's pace.

When I didn't feel God's guidance, it was because I let go of the wall. Because I was in the dark, I didn't know how close the wall was until I reached for Him. But there He was—only a touch away. I know that God is always with me, even when I don't feel His presence. But the darker and longer the tunnel, the closer I needed to keep to the wall. He was and still is my Rock.

It wasn't until after I was out of the tunnel that I looked back and saw a valuable lesson. By experiencing a relatively small dose of depression, now I could grasp what other people felt when they went through longer, darker tunnels than mine. I wasn't so quick to say, "Quit hurting. Everything will be fine." Pain is real. Problems hurt. There *is* a time for crying.

When I feel sorry for myself, I'm knocked back into reality by looking at what other people go through. I wouldn't want their problems. (Other people wouldn't want mine either.) We each have our own set of trials. It's not *what* problems we go through, its *how* we go through them. Romans 5:3 doesn't say to rejoice *because* of our problems, but to rejoice *in* them.

A friend of mine found a good way to get problems in the right perspective. She calls them C.B.'s, "Character Builders." When she's in the middle of a tough time, she can look at the trial objectively and with humor by calling it a C.B. Even her son uses it. After telling about his complicated problem, he said, "I know, Mom. You don't have to say it. It's just another C.B."

We all dread C.B.'s, but since they're a part of life, we might as well make the most of them. When we can't see anything good about what we're going through, at least we can grow on the inside because of it.

We lived in a rural community, so we hatched chickens in the second grade classroom where I taught. Some of the kids wanted to help the chicks hatch by pulling them out of their shells. I explained that a baby chick develops its muscles by struggling to get free from the shell. He looks pathetic, but the struggle makes him strong. When we go through hardships, we too struggle to be free of our problems, but the struggle makes us stronger on the inside.

God has His own way of using problems to build character in His children. We can't explain how He does it, but if we are in the right position with Him, God takes a bad situation and uses it for good (maybe so we can help someone else). Opening ourselves up to His transforming power keeps our eyes open for sprinkles of blessings in the middle of thunderstorms.

God doesn't *cause* my problems, but He *allows* me to go through them. As a parent, I don't cause problems to come to my child. I also don't protect him from all uncomfortable consequences. Should I do all his homework for him so he won't have to struggle? If he has a fight with a neighbor, should the family move to a new neighborhood? If he keeps breaking the same toy, do I keep replacing it? No. A good parent must *allow* his child to undergo a few hardships or he won't learn to interact, solve problems, and face reality.

When I have problems, it's hard to believe anything good is happening. I feel like a minus sign (−), lying flat on my face. But as I continue to reach up to God, the vertical connection to Him begins to transform the horizontal minus sign (−) into a plus sign (+). But sometimes the pluses I receive are not the ones I'm looking for. God has His own definition of changing problems into opportunities, pits into pedestals, dark into light. I don't know His timetable, but I know His presence. Other benefits may or may not appear, but His walking with me through the dark tunnel is the best plus I can have.

How does God make minuses into pluses? Through His Son, Jesus Christ. Take another look at your problems. You may be overwhelmed by your circumstances and see a minus sign. Or you may be dealing with your problems with a positive outlook and see a plus sign. But if you look at your problems through God's eyes, the plus sign becomes much more. You see the sign of His Son, not just a plus (+), but a cross (†).

FROM STRESS TO ACTION

Use your *Spiritual Notebook* for the following exercises.

❦ If you aren't sure of your position with God, clear up the relationship by praying through Romans 5:1-2. Use the exact Scripture, or put it in your own words. For example:

Dear God,
I believe that Jesus came to earth and died for me. I have done much that is wrong. These wrongs are against people, but most of all they come between me and a right relationship with You. Thank You that Your Son's death paid for all of these wrongs. I receive that gift of forgiveness and with it Your invitation to a right relationship with You. Thank You for the peace that this brings. Thank You for Your grace; I have done nothing to deserve a gift as great as Your forgiveness and this welcome into Your family. But I receive that gift with joy. It gives me hope for the future of my life—and for life even after death. You are a glorious God.

❦ On a page of your *Spiritual Notebook,* draw a cause-and-effect web of a current long-term problem or one you have already experienced. Put the problem in the center circle. Draw a line from the circle and say, "This caused me to. . . ." Draw another circle at the end of the line showing the effect. Draw a new line from the new circle and say, "This caused me to. . . ." Carry the web as far as you can. Effects could be good or bad, but ask God to stretch your perspective so you see at least one benefit from the difficulty. Consider the example on the next page.

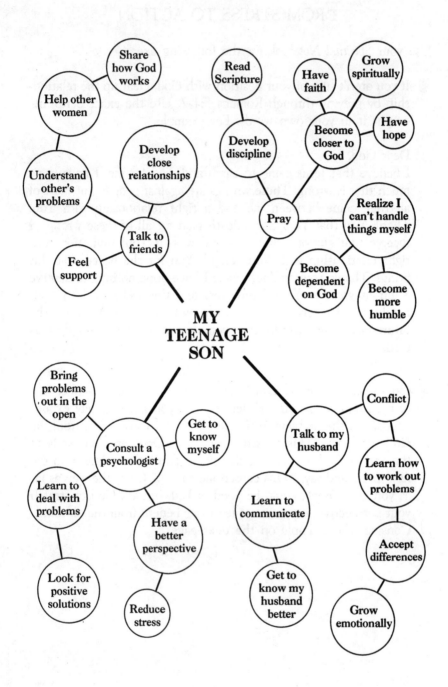

4

THE FACT IS...
De-Stress by
Using the Will

Psalm 22

Fʀᴏᴍ Sᴛʀᴇss ᴛᴏ Sᴏᴜʀᴄᴇ

Why me, Lord? Why is this happening to me? What did I do to deserve this? I thought You cared what happened to me. I thought You always watched over me. So why do I feel abandoned? How could You let this happen?

1. When and why have you felt like this?

How did your feelings reflect (or not reflect) a true picture of the situation?

2. Read Psalm 22. In this passage, David struggles between feelings and facts. He flip-flops between being stressed out and being spiritually strong. One minute he's beaten down, the next minute he's soaring upward. Label the following verses by whether they show fact or feeling. Then explain specifically what each fact or feeling is.

Verses	Fact or Feeling	Specific Fact or Feeling Shown
1-2	Feeling	Abandoned, Alone
3-5		
6-8		
9-10		
11-13*		
14-16*		
17-18		
19-21	David asks for God's help	
22-23		
24		
25-31		

* David uses metaphors (bulls, lions, dogs) to describe his enemies (NIV *Study Bible*).

3. Which verses show David's real turning point? What helped him come to this change of attitude?

4. In Psalm 22:3-5, how did David's remembering the past help him?

5. In Psalm 22:9-10, David remembers who God is to Him personally. What facts about God have you experienced and how would they help you deal with your problems?

6. In Psalm 22:11-13, David describes his enemies. How would you describe yours?

7. Is it right or wrong to express your true feelings to God? Explain.

8. In your opinion, can a person express his or her feelings too much? Why or why not?

9. In Psalm 22:19, David relies on these facts: God is near; God is his Strength. Because David knew these facts about God, he was able to seek God's help with confidence. What facts about God do you find in the following Scriptures? Notice how these same facts describe Jesus in the New Testament Scriptures.

❦ Deuteronomy 31:8; Matthew 28:20

❦ Deuteronomy 7:7-9; John 3:16; John 15:9.

❦ Revelation 4:8

❦ Psalm 34:8

❦ Psalm 86:5

❦ Psalm 100:5

10. In what specific situations do you find yourself emotionally distraught?

11. Which facts about God could be a turning point in your struggle?

12. How could these facts change your outlook?

13. What steps could you take to learn more facts about God? (For additional ideas, refer to *From Stress to Action*, activity 2.)

14. David takes his stand in Psalm 22:22. Would making such a commitment increase or decrease the stress in your life? Explain.

15. If your friend felt hopeless about a situation, what truth would you point her to? Which Scripture?

FROM STRESS TO STRENGTH

Choice. The word that divides right from wrong. The word posted on the crossroads of life. The word that carves character. The word that separates God's children from His enemies.

We choose to believe or to reject. To act or to turn our heads. To listen or disregard. To learn or ignore. We choose to change or not change. God gave everybody choices. That's what makes life so hard.

We are complex individuals, and how we choose to handle what's on the inside determines how we manage life on the outside. But what's going on inside of us? Why do some people have a grip on life and others struggle to survive?

Three forces are at work: the intellect, the emotions, and the will. At the risk of oversimplifying the process, let's look inside a person's inner being to understand these three dynamics.

Jessica. She is your neighbor. She is your boss. Jessica is David in Psalm 22. She is you. She is me. Inside Jessica's inner being, we see three characters that make up who she is. These characters constantly interact to determine how Jessica responds to her circumstances.

The first character inside Jessica is Intellectual Ivan. He lives by facts. He doesn't get bent out of shape because he sticks to what he knows is truth. The facts don't change much, so Ivan has a stable temperament—always knowing where he stands. Ivan is quiet, but solid. He is the logic in Jessica's mind. Intellectual Ivan isn't pushy, but when he takes charge of the inner being, he knows where he's going.

Emotional Ernie is the second character, the one who lives by feelings. His temperament surges up and down, depending on what's going on around him. When outside circumstances are good, Ernie feels great. When circumstances are bad, he is devastated. He's all passion. He makes life interesting, but sometimes Ernie becomes over-dramatic and selfish; he gets carried away with himself. Emotional Ernie is the loud one—the one Jessica hears first—the one that tries to control Jessica's behavior.

The third character in Jessica's inner being is Will. Jessica's Will is the essence of who she is, the master of the other two characters. Will is the center, the one who determines Jessica's thoughts, actions, and attitudes. He's the top banana. How Jessica uses Will determines who controls her thoughts: Intellectual Ivan or Emotional Ernie. As Jessica puts Will into action, she uses the God-given power of choice. Will keeps the balance between facts and feelings. Jessica's will is her choice of who she is.

Jessica has the choice of aligning her will with God's will. God reveals His truth to Jessica through her intellect as she reads about His wisdom, His faithfulness, and His care. It makes sense to trust such a God. But God also reveals His truth through Jessica's feelings. Sometimes Jessica can't logically explain why she knows—she simply feels God's truth. As Jessica grows in her faith, she learns to be sensitive to both her brain and her heart.

When she faces difficult problems, Jessica manages her stress level better when she controls her will. The power of decision is a source of great strength. Once she sets her will in a direction, Jessica's thoughts and feelings quit floundering, they fall in line with her decision. Her will determines her course—her attitude, her actions, and her future decisions. At times she will choose to live by facts, not feelings. At other times she will sense the "truth" that her feelings reflect. The choice is hers.

We'll learn more about Intellectual Ivan, Emotional Ernie, and Will if we see them in action. Enter Jessica's mind and watch the interaction of the three characters. Notice how stress is released as Jessica decides to align her will with what she knows is God's truth.

Jessica learns that her husband's company has transferred him to another state. They must move away from all their family and friends.

The news hits hard. Inside Jessica's inner being, Emotional Ernie goes to work, dominating Jessica's thoughts by reacting with her feelings. *This is terrible. I don't want to move away from all our friends. I'll never find a job as good as the one I have now. This home is all I know. Why do we have to move? We're happy here. I'll be all alone in a state I don't even like. How could God want me to leave my Bible study group? Why is this happening to me?*

Intellectual Ivan doesn't say much in Jessica's thoughts. He's very quiet about what he knows and doesn't argue with Ernie about it. (He knows Ernie has to go through his gyrations before he will listen to reason.) Ivan the Intellect realizes that Jessica is going to have to move to another state whether she likes it or not.

Inside Jessica's thoughts, Emotional Ernie goes on and on about feelings. In fact, the emotional side of Jessica dominates her thinking for two weeks, leaving her distraught, unable to sleep, angry at her husband, unable to function at work, and irritable with her children. Jessica's inner being is in turmoil because she gives Emotional Ernie full reign of her thoughts.

The next week, Jessica unloads her feelings onto a friend while they drive to Bible study. After listening to Jessica whine for thirty minutes, her friend looks her square in the face and says, "Jessica, what are your alternatives?"

"Well, just let me think about that a minute," Jessica replied.

Inside Jessica's mind, Intellectual Ivan perks up. This was the first time something factual had come into Jessica's mind since the news of the move. Intellectual Ivan takes a hard look at the reality of the situation and says through Jessica's voice, "I guess I could refuse to go . . . but that would destroy our family. I could insist that Mike find another job . . . but then I would be scared he couldn't find one. You know, I really don't have any good alternatives."

The friend quietly said, "Then you'll have to accept it."

Later, while the women discuss God's promises in the Bible study, a particular Scripture grabs Jessica's attention. She has read the verse before, but now it bolts out at her. "And we know that in all things God works for the good of those who love Him, who have been called according to His purpose" (Romans 8:28).

Ivan the Intellect speaks in Jessica's mind. "This is truth. You *know*, Jessica, that you love the Lord — that is a well established fact. You *know* that He has called you to be His child and He has always taken care of you in the past. Why should He quit now?"

Jessica begins to hear the facts in her inner being. They make sense, but she still feels crummy. How can she quit being over-whelmed by her feelings and start relying on facts? That's when Will comes to mind.

God gave Jessica the power of choice. He gave her a will. Jessica thinks over her situation, relying on facts Intellectual Ivan reveals to her. She sees that she is miserable while she listens to her feelings through Ernie. She turns to Will, the master of her inner being. What *should* she think?

Then it happens . . . a decision is made. Will takes control and chooses to listen to Intellectual Ivan instead of letting Emotional Ernie run wild with his feelings.

Jessica's decision to live by facts and not feelings gives her power over her circumstances. She can now accept the fact that she has to move. Deep down, Jessica knows God wants her to support her husband's decision to move because it is best for their family. Jessica chooses to put aside her feelings and align her will with God's. She knows God willtake care of her family wherever she is.

Jessica put Will into action, *choosing* to live by facts rather than feelings. When her feelings start clamoring, she quiets them by standing firmly on the facts and the power of her choice.

After Jessica's decision to accept the move, things changed. She began to support her husband, prepare her children for the move, gather information about jobs in the new city, and inquire about churches and Bible study groups. She moved into action.

The most amazing thing happened. Now that she was doing something positive toward the move, she didn't *feel* so bad about it. Inside, Emotional Ernie quit clamoring. Ernie even began to feel a little excited about the possibility of new friends and making a new home. (How quickly feelings change.)

The facts about the move remained the same. But the power of the will made the difference in Jessica's attitude and how she handled the situation. Once she took the step to align her will with the facts, her feelings fell into place.

When we feel down, distraught, discouraged, scared, unloved, or alone, we can allow Emotional Ernie to control us. Or we can look to Intellectual Ivan for facts. When we find something solid to base our beliefs on, we then need to give Will the power to control. We *are* what we *will*. God wants us—not just our thoughts and not just our feelings. If our will is aligned to His will, then we can truly say, "Thy will be done," knowing (and sometimes feeling) that we are on God's side.

When do we need to make a conscious effort to align our wills with God's? When we don't feel like it. When we are consumed by fear, doubt, and bitterness. When our circumstances make our emotions cry out in despair. When we can't forgive another person for hurting us. When we can't see anything good about a hopeless situation. When our world says, "That's impossible," and our God says "Believe it." When it's hardest to believe, that's when we need to *choose* to believe.

Am I saying that feelings are unimportant and they should be squelched? Not at all. Our emotions are an important part of our fiber. Our passion and sensitivity enables us to touch the lives of others and feel God's presence. God wants our passion. But when our emotions take over and cause harm to our inner beings—when feelings aren't kept in balance—when emotions paralyze us into inactivity—that's when it's time to re-focus on facts.

When I doubt, fear, or have negative thoughts, my feelings consume me. I want to believe that my teenage son is in God's hands, but the circumstances prove otherwise. When I can't believe, I say to myself, "I choose to believe." Saying this helps me trust that God is taking care of my son. Then my emotions don't run wild. I become empowered. When feelings scream at me to give up hope, facts calm me to trust. I choose to believe . . . and therefore I do believe. Ironically, I feel better when I decide to live on God's facts.

A common difficulty with new Christians is that when they have accepted Christ in their lives, they might not feel different. If Christians based their beliefs exclusively on how they felt, they wouldn't have much faith.

When I became a Christian, my friend helped me over this hurdle by showing me 1 John 1:5-10. She said if Jesus promised to live in my heart, then He would. Jesus didn't lie. If I doubted what He said, I called Him a liar.

That spoke to me. Who was I to tell Jesus He couldn't do what He promised? I began to look at the facts of what He said in the Bible and to stand on His Word. It didn't matter if I felt different or not. A fact is a fact. It doesn't change. Jesus lived in me whether I felt it or not because I made a decision to accept Him into my life. I chose Him with my will.

Make your decision. God gave you the power to use your will for His glory. You can live by feelings or facts. The choice is yours.

FROM STRESS TO ACTION

Use your Spiritual Notebook to:

❦ Describe how you would react to the following situations using your emotional side and then contrast it by using your intellectual side. Role play (on paper) *both reactions* for each of the following examples. Which do you think would be most helpful?

a. It's 2 a.m. Your teenager is two hours late. He finally walks in the door. What would you say if you responded emotionally? What would you say if you responded with facts? Which do you think would be the most helpful?

b. You are depressed because your best friend hasn't called you in two weeks.

c. Once again, you lost your temper with your two year old.

d. Your children have almost left the nest. You begin a career and are excited about a new purpose in life. Then you discover you are pregnant.

e. You offer yourself to God and want to follow Him. The same old sin keeps coming back to break your fellowship with Him.

f. Your mother-in-law becomes ill and you are the only one in the family who can take care of her. You can't afford outside help, so you must stay at home to nurse her.

g. Your boss asks you to take on an important project, but you already have two deadlines you are trying to make on other projects she has given you.

❦ Discover facts about God by examining Psalms 145–147. Find words about His character and what He does for us.

❦ Write a paragraph about who you are in relationship to God. This is the core of your belief system.

Note: Even the most mature Christians need to return to the basic facts about God when feelings are overwhelming. When your feelings are controlling your inner being, return to activities 2 and 3.

5

WHO, ME?
De-Stress by Loving

1 Corinthians 13

FROM STRESS TO SOURCE

If I am a dynamic speaker and travel around the world talking about Jesus, but I don't have love, I am only a loudspeaker's static or a noisemaker's racket. If I memorize all Scripture and understand every secret of God, if I have unshakable faith, if people come to me for prayer and discernment, if I have great insight and inspiration, but I don't have love, I am nothing. If I give a million dollars to the church and donate to every charity known, if I even give my own life to save another person, but I don't have love, I am worthless.

1. Read 1 Corinthians 13. What teachings do you find in this passage?

2. What gifts of the Spirit, or special abilities, does Paul mention in verses 1-3?

3. Why do you think God does not honor these gifts if the person doesn't have love?

4. Using 1 Corinthians 13:4-7 as a guide, describe a loving person. (Explain what a loving person does and does not do.)

5. Which of these descriptions is hardest for you to practice? Why?

6. How does stress interfere with practicing these loving qualities?

7. What practical steps could you take to prevent stress from affecting you in this way?

8. From the following Scriptures, show how Christ's life demonstrated the qualities of love that 1 Corinthians 13 describes.

   ❦ John 8:3-11

   ❦ Philippians 2:5-8

   ❦ Mark 8:1-3

   ❦ Mark 9:17-19

9. Think of some problems (either in your own life or someone else's). How could practicing the different qualities of love soften the effect of these problems? Be specific about which aspect of love would be practiced.

10. What if the person you are trying to love doesn't love you? How can you love someone who is unlovable?

11. Read Matthew 5:43-48. What challenges do these words present?

12. How would following Jesus' command help the other person?

13. How might following this command help us as well?

14. The Old and New Testaments are full of the same commands: Love the Lord your God and love your neighbor. Yet in John 13:34, Jesus says that He gives a new command. What is different about this one?

15. Why might receiving Christ's love help you to love someone who is hard to love?

16. In 1 Corinthians 13:8-12, what things will eventually become unnecessary? Why?

17. In your opinion, why is love considered greater than faith and hope?

18. Choose one way to practice love this week. How will you do it? (Ideas may come as you do *From Stress to Action*, activity 1.)

19. Think of an individual in your life who is hard to love. Who needs to change — you or the other person? What specifically can you do?

20. Describe unconditional love.

21. If you practiced 1 Corinthians 13, would it increase or decrease your stress level? Why?

FROM STRESS TO STRENGTH

"Mom, just stare at it for a long time and you'll see it," David said patiently.

I tried to see, but I couldn't grasp what my son saw in the three dimensional poster. We looked at the same picture. He saw dinosaurs; I saw dots. He saw living creatures; I saw patterns of color. He saw depth; I saw a flat surface.

"Look at your reflection on the glass and stare deep into the picture," David advised.

I stood for a long time looking *into* the dots of color. Then it happened. I saw! I stared in disbelief as the shapeless colors transformed into Tyrannosaurus Rex. The dinosaur glared back, almost laughing at me for not seeing him before.

Then I saw Stegosaurus and other dinosaurs emerge before my very eyes. I had a new vision. Dots were no longer flat. They took on new meaning when I saw them in the third dimension. Once I experienced this new sight, I could quickly get "into" all the other 3-D posters. I was blind, but now I could see.

My experience with the 3-D posters reminds me of 1 Corinthians 13:12: "Now I know in part; then I shall know fully, even as I am fully known." We see fragments of God through our limited human vision. In the future, however, we will see Him face to face in a new dimension. Only then will we fully understand the scope of His love and truly know Him.

God gave us glimpses of His love through His Son Jesus Christ. Two people stand side by side looking at the same Jesus. One sees a man. The other sees God. One sees a picture of flat colored circles. The other sees life itself in full dimension. One sees a man of compassion, strength, and wisdom. The other sees a God of holiness, grace, and power. Two people look. One is blind and the other sees.

Jesus told us over and over that He was God: "Anyone who has seen Me has seen the Father. . . . The words I say to you are not just My own. Rather, it is the Father, living in Me" (John 14:9-11).

We humans had God right before our eyes. We saw His love, His miracles, His forgiveness. We heard His teachings, His commands, His wisdom. But we killed Him. Human beings didn't have the vision to really see God until He was gone.

"For God so loved the world that He gave His one and only Son" (John 3:16). Jesus came to the world to reveal who God was and to show us His love.

What picture do you have of love? By today's standards, love is looking out for yourself. The world's love says, "I'll love you if you'll love me. I'll scratch your back if you'll scratch mine. If you really love me, you'll send me flowers. Do unto others as they do unto you."

But Paul painted a different picture of love in 1 Corinthians 13. He wrote about love that the world knows nothing about: unconditional love. The Bible's kind of love doesn't depend on whether the other person loves us back or not. God doesn't let us off the hook even when another person is cruel to us. He commands us to love that person anyway.

Why should we say "Good morning" to the coworker who spreads rumors about us? Why should we make a nice meal for the husband who forgets our anniversary? Why should we forgive the boss who made us feel like bread crumbs? Why? Because God told us to do it.

Why would God ask us to do something so hard? God commanded us to love each other, not so much for the other person's sake, but for ours. When we harbor hate toward someone, we spend "megahurts" of energy feeling sorry for ourselves. We become bitter. We hurt ourselves more than the one who has hurt us. What starts with a few bad feelings escalates to frustration, resentment, and stress.

Change must begin with us. When we decide to follow God's way, we put aside our own desires for revenge. We behave in a loving way to the other person, even if he doesn't deserve it. Loving our enemies goes against our grain, yet it's the best thing we can do for ourselves. We don't understand why, but we feel better when we love the other person in spite of that person's actions. The magic of love is that the giver is the receiver. Jesus did *us* a favor when He told us, in Matthew 5:43-48, to love our enemies. Hate imprisons us to bitterness, but love frees us to joy.

Love is easy to say, but hard to practice. Let's get real. We aren't going to be best friends with everyone we meet. Some personalities are like oil and water—they just don't mix. Some families are not the perfect breeding places for love. When we haven't been shown love, it's hard to know how to do it. Yet, Jesus' words are clear: Love those who are hard to love (Matthew 5:43-48). So how can we obey God's commandment when the other person is unlovable?

Do we try to make him lovable? We may try to change the other person, but reality slaps us in the face when we realize the other person *doesn't* change. We can only be responsible for our side of a relationship. We may not like what we see in the other person, but we can give him the right to be different from us. When we accept the fact that God made each of us different, we acknowledge the other person for who he is (even if we don't like *what* he is).

What if we can't make ourselves accept a particular person? Jesus thought of that problem too. He knew, with our limited view of love, we would have trouble loving the unlovable. So He gave us a new command (John 13:34-35). He told us to love like He loves—unconditionally.

God's love for us doesn't depend on how deserving we are. It's not a trade-off love. It's not a "show me and then I'll show you" kind of love. God's love is different from the world's love because it isn't based on "if."

We need to learn this new way of loving. How can we catch the vision of unconditional love? We could pretend that 1 Corinthians 13 is a picture of love on a 3-D poster. When we look at it in human dimension, we see inspiring words. But they remain flat on the pages of the Bible. The words sound too lofty to attain, too high to practice.

As we stare at 1 Corinthians 13 (as I stared at the 3-D posters), we look deeper into the passage and the words begin to transform into life. We no longer see patterns of color or impossible words to live. The picture of love emerges before our eyes in a new dimension. Jesus. Love becomes real when we see Christ practicing it. He walked it and talked it. Jesus was the perfect picture of love.

Christ modeled the love that Paul wrote about in 1 Corinthians 13. He had the ability to speak to the whole world and to the angels in heaven. But out of love, He talked to twelve men—and to you and me. He possessed all knowledge and understood God's purposes. He had supernatural power. But out of love, He shared the very heart of God with us. Jesus had faith to feed 5,000 people, give sight to the blind, and calm a storm. Out of love, He gave His all.

Jesus could have become an earthly king, but He died on a cross. Jesus could have thrown the first stone, but He saved a woman. Jesus could have dined with royalty, but He had dinner with a tax thief. Jesus could have stood on a pedestal, but He touched a leper. Jesus could have stayed by His Father's side, but He stepped down from His heavenly throne and became a baby in a manger. All this, for love.

The picture of love takes on great meaning when we see it in Christ's dimensions. Yet, Paul wrote 1 Corinthians 13 for us. How can we attain such a high standard of love? The Christ that lives within us wants out—out into the world where He can show His love. We are His vehicles, His tools, His communication with the world. He wants to live His love through our lives.

He doesn't expect us to be Him—we aren't God and we never will be. But in our realm of influence (with our families, coworkers, and neighbors) Jesus wants to show the world the real kind of love.

When we can't be patient, the Christ within us can. When we see the other person's faults, the Christ within us sees his strengths. When our feelings are hurt, the Christ within us forgives. When we are ready to give up on a person, the Christ within us hopes.

What do our 3-D posters of love look like when Christ is loving through us? Our actions are transformed into love of a new dimension. Love: a phone call, a smile, a pat on the back. Love: sitting by a hospital bed, building a snowman with a child, helping with homework. Love: saying "You can do it" or not saying a word. Love: not condemning our parents for their weaknesses, sometimes holding our tongues even when we know we're right. Love: letting the other person be different. Love: letting Christ shine in our lives.

When I couldn't see the 3-D poster in the third dimension, my son told me to stare at my own reflection until the images emerged. After staring for a long time, I saw.

Take a hard look at your own poster. What image do you reflect to others? Do they see the human dimension of your actions? Or when they look closely, do they see the reflection of Christ?

FROM STRESS TO ACTION

Use your *Spiritual Notebook* to do the following activities.

❦ 1 Corinthians 13:4-7 is a model for loving others. Write a specific situation where you could apply each phrase. For example: Love is patient: I could show patience when my family bothers me while I'm trying to write.

    (a) Love is patient
    (b) Love is kind
    (c) Love does not envy
    (d) Other

❦ Do you want to change your life? Memorize 1 Corinthians 13:4-7 and say it at least three times a day. After you are saturated with His Word, God will bring it to mind when you need it. Don't skip this activity even though it is difficult to do at first. Record exactly when you are going to say this passage during each day (In the shower, driving to work, at bedtime, other).

First Recitation:
Second Recitation:
Third Recitation:

6

NOBODY'S PERFECT
De-Stress by
Releasing Perfectionism

Philippians 3:1-16

FROM STRESS TO SOURCE

"Are you a good Christian?"

"I go to church every Sunday. Next month I'll receive my Twenty-Year Perfect Attendance Sunday School Award. I sing in the choir and take food to the needy every Christmas. I give money and follow all the rules in our church. I even repeat the Lord's Prayer every night. I'm sure God is proud of the good deeds I do. Yes, I'm a good Christian because I do all the right things."

Does following the letter of the law make you a good Christian? Christians of the first century must have asked the same question.

1. Read Philippians 3:1-16. What instructions does Paul give to Christians in this passage? (Draw from the whole passage.)

2. How could following these instructions de-stress your life?

3. What is the difference in being happy and rejoicing in the Lord?

4. How can you rejoice in the Lord even when bad things happen to you?

5. In Philippians 3:2, Paul blasted the Judaizers who preached that new Christians still needed to be circumcised—following the requirements of the old Hebrew law. According to verse 3, what are Paul's requirements for being a Christian? Explain what each one means to you.

6. Paul tells something of his own past in Philippians 3:4-6. How had Paul shown perfectionism in following the letter of the law?

7. What traps of legalism (acts of righteousness out of a sense of duty) do we fall into today?

8. In Philippians 3:7-9, Paul says that God has replaced the old way of being right with a new kind of righteousness. What is the difference in these two ways? (For further help, refer to *From Stress to Action*, activities 1 or 2.)

9. Why is it easy for us to fall into a self-righteous role, rather than to practice righteousness from Christ?

10. According to Philippians 3:10-11, what is Paul's goal?

11. What practical steps to know Christ can you take this week?

12. Even though Paul is a model Christian, he admits he isn't perfect in his daily walk. What is his technique for not becoming frustrated and throwing in the towel? (See verses 12-14.)

13. Paul sometimes "blew it" just as we do. According to verses 12-16, how do you think Paul would get back on track toward his goal?

14. What spiritual goal are you pressing toward?

15. What is your attitude when you begin to fall short of that goal?

16. How might this passage help you get back on track?

17. In view of Paul's words in the chapter to this point, what does Philippians 3:16 mean?

18. When do you think perfectionism crosses the line from being beneficial to being a hindrance?

19. In what areas do you let your own perfectionism be a problem to yourself or to others? (Follow up by doing *From Stress to Action,* activity 3.)

20. What steps could you take to keep the proper perspective in these areas?

FROM STRESS TO STRENGTH

I answered the door and found two small neighborhood girls standing with big grins on their faces. Each of them clutched several pieces of paper.

"Do you want to buy our pictures?" they asked.

I looked at the primitive artwork of the five year olds and smiled. The girls explained the different prices for each picture. As I paid each of them a dollar for their masterpieces, their eyes gleamed with excitement. They had actually sold their works of art.

Why did I buy their drawings? Did I look at the quality of the artwork? Did I compare the pictures with other paintings in my home?

Was the product really worth the money?

No. I paid the price because of who the girls were—not the drawings. I didn't care what the pictures looked like. I bought the pictures for the people, not the product.

In the same way, God looks at our inadequate artwork. He smiles and buys our childish drawings when nobody else will. He accepts our meager works with open arms because of who we are in His family. In fact, He paid a big price for us 2,000 years ago—He paid for us with His only Son, Jesus Christ.

God loves us and accepts us for who we are, not for what we do. We could never do anything to impress a God who created life inside a human body. A God who made the mountains and oceans. A God who keeps multitudes of stars and planets in perfect order. A God who knows how many hairs are on each of our heads. What could we possibly do for such a God?

We can't impress Him, but we can please Him. He smiles at us when we offer ourselves for His service. He knows our human limitations so He looks at our hearts—not the quality or the quantity of our works. He accepts our acts of love because He accepts us.

Sometimes we confuse what God values. He calls us to a high standard of values and morals. He wants us to do the right things. But He wants the person first and then our good works. We sometimes get things backward and try to work for God's approval instead of trusting in His acceptance.

Even if our good works help other people, God doesn't accept them if our hearts have the wrong motive. Acts of service done only in our own strength don't set well with our Father. Self-centered or self-motivated acts twist themselves into self-righteousness and "Holier than Thou" thinking (not a pretty sight in God's eyes).

God looks for the heart that is Christ-centered. He accepts works that serve His purposes. He searches for the one who has compassion for others. He calls us to be righteous, but He won't allow us to become smug about doing His business. God wants the credit. He calls us to faith in Christ's righteousness, not our own. (See Romans 3:21-28.)

High standards, goals, and conscientiousness are desirable qualities, but if we become paralyzed by them, our lives get stressful. When high standards become too lofty, perfectionism can cripple our efforts. The student who turns in his term paper late because it isn't perfect; the artist who doesn't show his work because he sees flaws; the homemaker who doesn't invite friends over for dinner because she can't get the house, dinner, and family perfect all at the same time; the Christian who lives in defeat because he can't walk the talk—all are victims of perfectionism.

When doing our best keeps us from doing anything at all, it's time to loosen up. Our strength becomes our weakness. When excellence tips the scales and becomes overbalanced with perfectionism, life becomes stressful for us and for the people around us. It can happen to me, to you, or to someone you know.

I once had a student who suffered from a bad case of perfectionitis. "Greg" had trouble with a lot of things in school, but he was a great artist. When other children traced dinosaurs, Greg free-handed his dino to perfection.

"What a great dinosaur. It looks just like the one in the book," the other students and I praised Greg for his artistic ability.

Everything went great until Greg failed to shade the picture the way he wanted. Before I realized what he was doing, he tore up the picture and threw it on the floor. If he couldn't make it perfect in his eyes, he didn't want it at all. All-or-nothing thinking prevented Greg from succeeding in an area in which he could have excelled.

When a baby is born into a family, his parents see him as perfect. But what can he do? He only eats, sleeps, cries, and wiggles. He has the potential to walk, talk, interact with others, and become a purposeful individual. But the infant can't do any of those things. He only lies in his bed, unable yet to perform the functions for which he was made.

Do we look at a baby and think how imperfect he is because he doesn't act like an adult? Of course not. We ooh and aah over how perfect he is. His birth is only a beginning, the first stage for developing into a purposeful person.

Does the infant strive for perfection as he learns life's skills? No, the baby doesn't wait until he can win the 100-yard dash before he takes his first step. He pushes forward and he falls. He tries again, but fails. Although the baby doesn't attain perfection, he keeps trying until he walks. Does he feel frustrated with his mistakes? Sometimes. But he's not afraid to fail because his parents praise him for trying. They know he will eventually learn, so they aren't upset with his imperfections. In fact, parents accept an infant's failure as a natural process of learning.

God is our parent. He looks at us as if we are infants, toddlers, adolescents, mature adults, or senior citizens going through different stages of faith. He understands that we are in a process.

After all, He made us. He's the Father and His job is to teach, train, guide, protect, and discipline us (just as we do for our children). God sees us as perfect in whatever stage we are in.

If there's no need to be perfect, why do we get hung up on it? Fear. We're afraid someone will see us for who we really are. If we aren't sure about our own self-worth, we can't stand to wear our mistakes on the outside so others will see them. We strive for the flawless, the complete, or the precise so others won't see us in a bad light. Sometimes individuals who need to have everything perfect don't trust their own capabilities. They constantly reinforce their self-worth by what they do. This is when perfectionism becomes a disease.

Medicine for perfectionitis: Face the worst thing that could happen if you blow it. What happens if the straight A student makes a B? (It takes the pressure off.) What happens if you can't get the laundry done one week? (The family learns you're human and not super-mom.) What happens if you can't get the work project organized? (You ask for help and other people become responsible too.) The world goes on, even if you make a mistake or don't live up to your expectations.

There's nothing wrong with having high standards and goals — if we don't become obsessed by them. We need to have a sense of satisfaction with a job well done. We should be our own cheerleaders. But if we're rigid, inflexible, and have inflated expectations, we won't be content with the results or with ourselves. Trying to be perfect causes stress. Our efforts are never enough. Good always could be better. Nothing quenches the thirst for needing to do more. Self-worth becomes based on what we accomplish, rather than on who we are.

Kitty, a friend of mine, told me her husband set out to clean the outside of the electric skillet. (You know all those brown spots that never come out?) He scrubbed for hours, but he couldn't remove every stain. His intensity amazed Kitty. She said, "Just think of the time and energy he wasted. And the skillet still has brown spots. As long as the inside is clean, who cares about the outside?"

That's how God looks at us as we try to look shiny on the outside. He knows we waste our time and energy trying to do the impossible. What He cares about is on the inside.

Perfectionism can be simply a part of a person's personality. Some folks "hang loose" while others "cling tight." It's not bad to be a conscientious person (we need these types to manage the world). If you have a precise, meticulous disposition, make the most of it by offering your strengths where needed. But learn to bend a little when dealing with other people, and don't be too hard on yourself. A fine line separates high quality and over-perfectionism.

We can also impose our perfectionism on other people without them even knowing it. Have you ever put people on a pedestal? I've done this several times, and I have always been disappointed. When the people didn't live up to my expectations, I felt hurt and betrayed. Now I realize that it was my fault (in part) for expecting them to be perfect. I should have respected them for themselves — just as they were. It wasn't their fault if they fell off my pedestal because I'm the one who put them there. They probably didn't even know I held them in such impossible esteem.

If I'm looking for somebody to idolize, I need to look at Jesus — He'll never let me down. The only entity that is perfect is God (Father, Son, and Holy Spirit).

Many Indian tribes have a beautiful custom of acknowledging the perfection of God. If they weave a basket without making a mistake, they purposely create a flaw in it because they know that God alone is perfect. According to this tradition, perfection is saved for the Holy One.

Contrary to this Indian custom, our society pushes for good, better, and best. We live in a performance-based social order, especially with today's technology and information capacity. Would a manufacturer purposely create a flaw in a product to acknowledge that only God is perfect? Humility is a foreign word to us. Yet, when we compare ourselves to God's perfect qualities and Christ's sinless life, we must fall to our knees.

If you want to reduce stress in your life, look at the process, not the product. Improve your inner being, and you will like your outer actions. Let God make you perfect in His own way, in His own time. Instead of setting your goal on the top rung of the ladder, reach for the one just above your head. When you achieve that height, you can feel satisfied as you reach for the next rung. God is happy with you if you keep climbing toward Him. God knows you're not perfect, but you *are* perfectly made.

FROM STRESS TO ACTION

Use your *Spiritual Notebook* to do one or more of the following activities:

❦ Read Hebrews 7:11-28. Write a paragraph explaining what this passage means to you. Contrast the imperfect old law with the new covenant of Jesus.

❦ Pretend you are explaining Romans 3:21-28 to a child. What would you say?

❦ Ask God to show you areas in which you need to release perfectionism. Pray about these things every day for two weeks. Write specifics down in your *Spiritual Notebook*. Be open to His leading.

7

A NEW WORD—NO!
De-Stress by Setting Limits

Exodus 18

FROM STRESS TO SOURCE

The Press Secretary forced the White House doors open against the crowd. He clutched the microphone and announced, "The time is 5:00 a.m. and the President of the United States will now see the first parties in disagreement. The rest should take a number and form a line starting at the White House door and continuing down Pennsylvania Avenue. The President will settle your disagreements one at a time from now until midnight. Please be patient as you wait your turn. If you don't see the President today, come back tomorrow."

As absurd as this scenario sounds, this was exactly what Moses did with the Israelites. Perhaps you and I are also guilty of trying to perform impossible tasks. Not setting limits drives stress to a peak.

1. Read Exodus 18. What lessons did Moses need to learn?

2. How could these lessons help de-stress your life?

3. Why do you think that Moses sent his wife, Zipporah, to her father? (See verses 1-2.)

4. In view of the rest of the passage, write a paragraph about what Zipporah might have told her father.

5. Review verses 1-12. What do these verses tell you about Moses' father-in-law?

6. Describe the relationship between Jethro and Moses.

7. What problems did Jethro bring to Moses' attention in verses 13-18?

8. Why was Moses' system hard on the people?

9. Focus on verses 19-23. What solution did Jethro offer to Moses?

10. Would you have followed Jethro's advice? Why or why not?

11. Why did Moses feel responsible for the people? (Refer to Exodus 3:12-15 and 18:15.)

12. Do you think Moses was "playing God"? Explain.

13. How do we get trapped into assuming too much responsibility for others at home? At work? At church?

14. In which areas of your life do you feel indispensable? (If these are causing your stress, refer to *From Stress to Action*, activity 1.)

15. Do you like feeling indispensable? Why or why not?

16. Is it hard for you to ask for help? Explain.

17. When someone helps you, do you want to continue to be involved? Or do you want someone else to take *total* control? Why?

18. How are the people around you affected when you are involved in too many activities?

19. Reread verses 24-26. What wisdom do you see in Moses' actions here?

If you had been Moses, what type of person would you choose to help you?

20. Do you think that Moses would choose you? Why or why not?

21. What are some vital reasons for saying "no" when asked to do a job?

22. What are some vital reasons for saying "yes"? (Apply this by doing *From Stress to Action*, activity 4.)

FROM STRESS TO STRENGTH

"Jesus, be our king. We have waited too long for someone to over-power this government."

"That is not My purpose."

"Jesus, be our healer. You could heal hundreds every day. There would be no more sickness."

"That is not My purpose."

"Jesus, be our miracle worker. You can feed 5,000 people with two fish, turn water into wine, and even calm the storms. There's no end to what you could do for us."

"That is not My purpose. I came to save the world from sin."

Jesus knew His purpose. He knew who had sent Him and why. He knew where He had come from and where He was going. He possessed the power to set people free of injustices, cure the world of sickness, and right all the wrongs. But God sent His Son with a mission to accomplish. Jesus lived on earth for one purpose — to die.

He died so we could live. Would Jesus, being a man of compassion, want to heal each blind person that begged for sight? Would a man of mercy want to reach out and touch each leper that looked into His eyes for a restored life? Would a man of righteousness, such as Jesus, want to overthrow an unfair government and replace it with a system that would be equal to all? Would a man who knew He faced death want to hide from the men that planned to kill Him? Would an innocent man want to defend himself against false accusations?

Of course He would. Jesus was as much man as He was God. Imagine the frustration He felt. Jesus could free people from their misery, but He had to die. He could have worn a royal crown, but He wore one of thorns.

Jesus could have settled for man's way, but He chose God's. The man in Jesus wanted to please the crowd, but the God in Him said, "No." The man in Him wanted to go a different route, but the God in Him said, "Go this way." The man in Jesus wanted to stay with His friends, but the God in Him kept divine appointments with strangers.

We must choose too—our way or God's. The self in us longs to do one thing, and God in us demands another. How can we develop the same goals as God sets for us? By modeling Jesus.

How did Jesus stick to His purpose without being sidetracked? Was He pre-programmed like a robot? How did He know which events were planned by His Father and which ones were distractions from men?

Mark 1:32-39 shows Christ's secret for connecting with His Father. Jesus held the entire city of Capernaum in the palm of His hand. His ministry held a foretaste of success. After a night of peak performance, the disciples were ready for more action the next day. "Where's Jesus? Doesn't He know the people are waiting for Him? He's got a lot of folks to heal today."

When the disciples found Jesus, they exclaimed, "Everyone is looking for you!"

Imagine their surprise when He said, "Let's go somewhere else."

Why did Jesus leave? Because He consulted His Commander, received His marching orders, and obeyed. In Mark 1:35, Jesus didn't receive the instructions by osmosis. He deliberately withdrew from His followers so that He could pray. Jesus needed time to connect with His Father, listen, and follow the orders. (That doesn't sound very different from what we need to do.)

Jesus may have wanted to stay at Capernaum and heal the entire city, but God told Him to move on. So He did. No excuses. No promises to be back. He simply moved on.

Sometimes I twist my prayers to fit my own agenda. I decide what I want to do and then say, "Lord, bless my actions. Give me the strength to carry out my will."

I will never know the joy of obedience until I ask the Master what He wants. He anxiously waits for me to say the magic words: "Lord, use me." Then He knows I'm ready for service—His service. If I don't ask, I don't want to know.

Ephesians 2:10 states, "For we are God's workmanship, created in Christ Jesus to do good works, which God prepared in advance for us to do." God has His own agenda for us. He prepares marching orders for us just as He did for Jesus. He plans particular people for us to touch, certain words that only we can say, acts of kindness that only *we* can perform. He commissions us for His work, not our own.

Several years ago I wanted to lead a weekly women's Bible study which would take many hours of weekly preparation. Along with my teaching career, I belonged to several educational and social groups. My life was already crammed to the top of the barrel. My wise husband said he thought that if I led the Bible study, I should drop all other extra activities.

I felt devastated. What would my friends think of me for being a quitter? I had been a faithful member of one teachers' organization for fifteen years. How could they get along without me? They did.

I discovered that it wasn't hard to give up something I had previously enjoyed because now I had a different purpose. God changed my priorities and caused me to let go of my old patterns and develop new ones. Being flexible to God changed me. I learned that if I know why I'm living, then I know *how* to live.

Moses had a bad case of the "all" disease. He carried the people on his shoulders for forty years. They looked to him for leadership and wisdom. He was the voice of God to them. Moses was a great man, but he wasn't God. It took an outsider like his father-in-law, Jethro, to see what Moses could not see.

Sometimes we "play God" without realizing it. When we're in the middle of a fire, we see only the flames. Someone on the outside can reach in and show us the way out of danger because he sees the problem from a different angle. Jethro rescued Moses from the fire of overwork and kept him from total burn-out (no pun intended). Jethro offered sound, godly advice and Moses accepted it. When Moses shared the responsibilities, the system worked. New leaders emerged and met the people's needs. And Moses wasn't stressed out.

When we spread ourselves too thin, we are like a painter using one can of paint for the entire house. We cover a lot of surface, but it doesn't do any good because our paint isn't thick enough to penetrate the boards. We only hit the high spots. As our paint runs out, we water it down and keep painting . . . thinner . . . thinner . . . and thinner. Finally, there's no more paint. We look at the empty can and the unfinished house. It looks as if we smeared shoe polish over the boards. We sigh, looking at our wasted effort. Too little spread too far. We won't hear the words, "Well done, my good and faithful servant."

God has a plan. He may want me to paint one side of the house and you to paint another. He may want both of us to work on the same side. Maybe He wants me to work long hours and then rest while someone else works.

When God is in charge, He will supply all the paint we need. The can will never run dry. By each of us doing a good job at what He directs (and not trying to paint the whole house by ourselves), we will do His will. The house will be thoroughly painted and God will get the credit for knowing how to get the job done.

We are His painters, but He's the one in charge. Ephesians 2:9 says, "not by works, so that no one can boast." He wants us in our proper places — on our knees before the Almighty God.

It's scary to drop our own goals and seek what God wants us to do. What if He doesn't use us? What if we don't like His plans? What if we feel that we're inadequate for the job?

God shares His heart in Jeremiah 29:11-13: "For I know the plans I have for you," declares the Lord, "plans to prosper you and not to harm you, plans to give you hope and a future. Then you will call upon Me and come and pray to Me, and I will listen to you. You will seek Me and find Me when you seek Me with all your heart."

If you believe this promise from God, would you set limits on your *own* plans so you would have time to discover His plans? Would you take a risk and say, "Lord, I am at Your service today. Use me however You like"? Would you use the word "no" to the world, so you could say "yes" to God?

FROM STRESS TO ACTION

Use your *Spiritual Notebook* to:

❦ Pinpoint one area of your life that you need to simplify. Write a plan of improvement. If you have trouble doing this task, ask a close friend to help you see it objectively. Consider the following: (1) Problem? (2) Tasks you must do? (3) Tasks others could do to help? (4) Who could help? (5) Would they help? If not, how could you approach them with the possibility? (6) Does God want you to change this area?

❦ Return to chapter 2 on Priorities in your *Spiritual Notebook*. Any changes? Adjust, if necessary.

❦ Write three good qualities about yourself. Write ways God might use these qualities.

❦ The concept of letting God plan our day sounds good on paper, but does it really work? Start your day with prayer. Think of good things about God and tell Him. Then think through your activities for the day. Ask God to help you do the things *He* wants, even if it means changing your routine. As you go through your day, ask Him if you are following what He wants. Look for His leading in little things too. If you see no difference, do it again the next day. Relax and let God work in your daily schedule.

8

KEEPING FIT
De-Stress by
Practicing Good Habits

1 Thessalonians 5:12-24

FROM STRESS TO SOURCE

If you wrote your prayers, could you call your notebook a *daily* prayer journal? Or would your pages have big gaps of time in them like this?

January 1
    Dear Heavenly Father, I feel so close to You. I want to follow You every day of this new year. . . .
February 1
    Dear Heavenly Father, what's wrong with me? Why do You seem so distant?

1. Read 1 Thessalonians 5:12-24. Using the entire passage, summarize in several sentences the instructions Paul gives to help us live a consistent, Christian life.

2. Notice how many absolutes (words like "all," "never," "everybody,") are found in these verses. Why do you think Paul uses such strong words?

3. Focus on 1 Thessalonians 5:12-15. Which of these instructions would be the most difficult for you to practice? Why?

4. List several spiritual leaders. (People who influence in some way the spiritual development of your life.)

5. How could you follow these instructions if you disagreed with one of these leaders on a spiritual question?

6. What specific ways can you practice 1 Thessalonians 5:12-15 in your church or cluster of Christian friends?

7. In what specific ways could you practice these instructions in your family?

8. How might Paul's instructions in 1 Thessalonians 5:16-18 help you manage stress?

9. How can you pray continually and still work, raise a family, and perform daily tasks?

10. How can you thank God even in difficult circumstances?

11. How did you handle the last difficult circumstance you had?

12. In view of this passage, how might you handle the next one?

13. Do you think that Paul is telling us to deny reality by practicing these verses? Why or why not?

14. In 1 Thessalonians 5:19-22, what additional instructions does Paul give about spiritual growth?

15. Verse 19 says, "Do not put out the Spirit's fire." In what ways do you think we might stifle the Holy Spirit?

16. How can we fan the fire of the Holy Spirit in ourselves?

17. Verse 21 warns us to "test everything." How can we test new teaching?

18. Verse 22 tells us to "avoid every kind of evil." Where do you see evil? How can you avoid it?

19. What encouragement do you find in 1 Thessalonians 5:23-24?

20. If you try to follow all these instructions to the best of your ability, what will keep you from wearing down?

21. Verse 16 invites us to "be joyful always." In view of this whole passage, what is the difference in self-generated joy and joy that is the result of the Holy Spirit?

22. List specific ways you can keep spiritually fit.

23. What is one spiritual exercise you would like to take on this week?

FROM STRESS TO STRENGTH

It's Monday . . . a day for new beginnings. Starting today I will live a balanced life. I'm getting into a routine and doing all the things I know are good for me. I am determined to be physically, intellectually, emotionally, and spiritually fit.

I'd better put in a load of laundry before I start my routine. Uh, oh. *The phone's ringing.*

"Mom, I forgot my saxophone and the bus leaves at 11:00 for the band contest. Could you bring it to me, please?"

"OK, son. I'll be right there."

Oh, dear. There's the phone again.

"Diane, I'm so glad you're home. I'm trying to make a decision. Do you have time to listen?"

"I'll drop by your house after I run by the school."

(Two hours later.) Now maybe I can start my routine. There it is again. Will the phone ever quit ringing?

"Honey, Rick just called and said he and Michelle will be in town for the evening. I hope it's all right that I invited them over for dinner. If it's not, I'll call him back."

"It'll be fine. We haven't seen them in a year. I'll figure out something to make for dinner."

Now where was I? Oh, yes. I was becoming physically, intellectually, emotionally, and spiritually balanced.

Oh, well. Maybe tomorrow.

When the unexpected happens, what's the first thing to go? When push comes to shove, what do you ditch? If you're anything like me, you find yourself eating in the car, staying up late, and not exercising. Praying becomes too time consuming to fit in.

Unexpected daily interruptions are bad enough, but what happens when you get "big time" stress? What activities do you skip when the unexpected heart attack comes, when you lose your job after twenty years with a company, when your husband announces that you're not young enough for him anymore, when the doctor says that your baby will live, but will always be handicapped? What do you throw out, and what do you keep during these crash periods?

Most experts agree that rest, exercise, meditation, and healthy eating habits help fight the battle with stress. Sound familiar? The very things that help me deal with stress are the ones I throw out the window when things get tight.

Life calls me to put out fires. Some are small grass fires, and some are infernos. Firemen wouldn't rush into the blaze without proper equipment and neither should we.

Firemen expect fires. They prepare for them by practicing emergency drills over and over. They don't wait until the alarm rings to learn how to handle the hose. Firemen strengthen and train their muscles well in advance of the emergency. They practice for the crises.

Just as firemen expect fires, we should expect stress. It's not a matter of *if* we have stress, but *when* we have it. We can't wait until we're in the middle of a fire to practice our drills and to build our muscles. We need to follow Paul's instructions in 1 Thessalonians 5:12-24 during the good times so that when the bad times come, we will have tools and protection to fight the fires. Even though we can never prepare fully for the unexpected, we can train our spiritual muscles and use God's equipment. Sometimes following a well-established routine is the only thing that carries us through the crisis.

Several years ago a fire broke out next door to my parents' house. Because I live down the street from them, I panicked when I saw smoke coming from that direction. My heart pounded as my husband and I ran down the street to their house. Fear hit me as I saw flames shoot into the air. While the firemen fought the blaze next door, we hosed down my parents' roof to prevent the fire from spreading to their house. I shook for hours after the ordeal was over.

A few months later, a house located behind my parents' house, caught fire. (Two fires in one block was very unusual.) Our family proceeded through the same routine of hosing down my parents' roof—just as we did for the first fire. After it was over, my father and I both commented that we didn't panic during this second fire. We knew what to do and we did it. Even though the fire was an emergency, there was a sense of calm about it just because we knew the routine.

Practicing 1 Thessalonians 5:12-24 gives me a routine of positive living that helps me fight the fires of stress. Carrying out the routine of good habits stabilizes me when everything else is falling apart. But I can't wait until I'm in the middle of a crisis to establish these good habits.

Many will read Paul's instructions and think, "Good idea, Paul. If I could live like that, I wouldn't have any stress in my life. It sounds good, but fat chance that I could ever do all those things." Then they will move on with their lives, leaving the words lifeless on the pages of their Bibles. Many will read, but few will do.

Perhaps ten who read this passage will let the words mull over in their minds. They will begin to think what it would be like if they practiced keeping peace, rejoicing, and praying continually. These ten women will pump energy into the ideas. The words will take shape (different shapes for different personalities and different circumstances). These ten brave individuals will water and feed the ideas until the words take root and bud into an action. When words transform into action, change takes place.

The ten women who experience this change will eventually be faced with a crisis. The unexpected comes and throws them off-guard. The circumstance will pull them into a pattern of pain, and some will forget the words that once gave them strength. They will wonder where God is during this time of trouble. Circumstances will rob them of their joy.

But out of these ten people of action, perhaps one woman will continue to water and feed the new shoots of growth, even when things get tough. The hardest time to cling to God's truth is when she needs it most. Bad habits will creep in after a few weeks, but this rare individual will weed them out and make room for the new patterns she is putting into action. She will dig, prune, and loosen the soil. The good habits will flourish and become stronger even during the dry periods. Her perseverance will hold her close to the words that give her strength.

If she keeps on "keeping on," her actions will become habits and she will automatically practice the words that are ingrained within her. Good habits are as hard to break as bad habits. Habits, good or bad, are what she lives.

As the words become alive in her daily routine, this rare woman will sense a new rhythm to her life. The new patterns of thinking will begin to change her attitudes and how she handles problems.

When she reads in 1 Thessalonians 5:12 that she should respect her spiritual leaders, she becomes more teachable and open to change in her life. She really listens and tries to apply new lessons.

When she reads in 1 Thessalonians 5:14 about how she should relate to those around her, she gets involved in other people's lives and not so caught up in her own needs. Her daily life becomes a Christ-like illustration to others.

When she reads in 1 Thessalonians 5:16 about how to keep herself strong in the Lord, she conducts the activities of her day with an attitude of prayer all day long. When difficult circumstances scream at her to deny the words, this woman retains some elements of inner peace.

When she reads in 1 Thessalonians 5:19 about how she should not put out the Spirit's fire, she rekindles the Spirit's sparks as she tests each new truth and makes room for new seeds to grow. Her spiritual life becomes an adventure.

When she reads in 1 Thessalonians 5:23 about how God sanctifies her, she knows that God is making His Word grow within her. Her good habits of watering and feeding don't cause the growth. God is the One who grows the seeds—the woman is just the gardener.

Many read these words from Paul's letter to the Thessalonians, but few live them. Many people walk through the garden "oohing and aahing" over the beautiful flowers. But there are only a few who will roll up their sleeves and dig into the soil. God is looking for gardeners, not gawkers.

> *The woman who reads the words*
>   *changes her moment.*
> *The woman who forms the words into ideas*
>   *changes her thoughts.*
> *The woman who puts the ideas into action*
>   *changes her day.*
> *The woman who repeats actions to form habits*
>   *changes her life.*

God has given us the words of the Bible. Most of us will read them and leave them. But ten of us will put them into action. One of us will make them a part of our daily lives. Will you be the one?

FROM STRESS TO ACTION

Use your *Spiritual Notebook* to:

🐛 Write a paragraph about what Matthew 22:37-39 means to you.

🐛 Brainstorm ways to keep physically, intellectually, emotionally, and spiritually fit. Write several notes under each area.

Choose one activity from each area to put it into action this week. If you write the habit you are going to form, your chances of carrying it through will be doubled. You will become one of the ten women who puts words into actions.

If you want to become the *one* woman who sticks to it and changes her habits, post your commitment in a prominent place. The paper will remind you of your goal throughout the day. The woman who actually takes these steps will change her life. Will it be you?

To keep physically fit, I will _____

To keep intellectually fit, I will _____

To keep emotionally fit, I will _____

To keep spiritually fit, I will _____

    Signed _____
            (One committed woman)

77

INTRODUCTORY MEETING

OBJECTIVE
To understand that the study is based on applying what we learn.

Note: The original "de-stress" group met bimonthly for an hour and a half. If your group's time together is more brief, the leader will need to select questions from those listed in each *Group Time.* In spite of time constraints, try to keep the opening activity for each lesson. This bridge into the study will help the members feel comfortable with each other and prepare them for the study ahead. The emphasis of this introductory study is to encourage each other to grow and to *practice* what is discussed. Be sure that you become familiar with the *From Stress to Action* section of each chapter and also learn how to create a *Spiritual Notebook.*

LEADER PREPARATION
- Pray for each woman who will be in the group.
- Bring a copy of *De-Stressing Your Life* for each woman.
- Bring small pieces of paper, pencils, and a basket.
- Bring three-ringed binders (with dividers for each chapter) for each member. Labels should be: Praying, Priorities, Perspective, Using the Will, Love, Releasing Perfectionism, Setting Limits, Good Habits.

GROUP TIME
1. Allow time for each woman to briefly tell something interesting about herself. She might tell about her family, job, or why she came to the group.

2. Pass out several squares of paper to each person. "Write all the things that stress you out (one on each paper) and put the squares in the basket." As the leader draws each paper out of the basket, the group gives the source of stress a category. (Examples: family relationships, household responsibilities, career, health, social activities, miscellaneous.) By classifying the subjects, the group can easily see common sources of stress.

3. Is stress in our lives always bad? How could pressure help us?

4. Hand out copies of *De-Stressing Your Life.* Invite your group to look at the table of contents. Then point out and explain the sections dividing each chapter. (See pages 5–6.)

5. Explain: "The main emphasis of this study is to practice what we learn. A valuable tool for applying new truth in our lives is a Spiritual Notebook." (Distribute binders.) "Each chapter of the text book has a closing section called *From Stress to Action.* Keep a record in your notebook of your progress through these activities. Then bring it to each meeting for discussion. You can also use your notebook to journal prayers, record favorite Scriptures, and target personal insights."

6. Since *From Stress to Action* is the most important part of each lesson, each woman should make an effort to complete the lesson early in the week. The weekly study can be divided into:

    Day 1–2   *From Stress to Source* (Study)
    Day 3   *From Stress to Strength* (Reading)
    Day 4–6   *From Stress to Action* (Applying)
    Day 7   Reviewing and Reflecting

7. Explain that this study is focused on taking steps, not reaching the impossible goal of a stress-free life. Through open and honest discussions, we will all learn from each other.

8. Pray that this study will make a difference in each life this week.

Group Study 1

TAKE IT, GOD
De-Stress by Praying

Philippians 4:4-13

OBJECTIVE
To release anxieties to God through prayer.

LEADER PREPARATION
- Complete all activities in chapter 1.
- Bring Post-it notes to the meeting.
- Be prepared to share something for which you could have thanked God during a time that your prayers didn't seem to be answered.
- If your time is limited, select from the list below which questions you will use. (See note in *Introductory Meeting.*)

GROUP TIME
1. Pray a short opening prayer with Matthew 11:28-30 in mind.
2. Think of your stress level as a thermometer ranging from 1–10. (Ten is stressed out.) What is your stress temperature this week? What areas are affecting your level?
3. At the top of a Post-it note, write your biggest stress-producer. Put it aside until the close of the session.
4. Read Philippians 4:4-13. What instructions in these verses could reduce stress?
5. According to this passage, what benefits can result from following these instructions?
6. What does practicing these truths reveal about God? What does it reveal about us?
7. Describe a time when you didn't receive what you asked for in prayer. In retrospect, what could you thank God for now?

8. Why do you agree or disagree with the concept: God's job is to work and our job is to trust.

9. How could thanking God before you see the answer stretch your faith?

10. What people are in your network of support? How do they help you?

11. How can you support other people?

12. Study Philippians 4:8-9. What are some ways that you could put Paul's instructions into practice?

13. What method did you use this week to keep your mind focused on good things? How did it work? (Refer to your *Spiritual Notebook*.)

14. Look at your *Spiritual Notebook* and *From Stress to Action*, question 3. Did a particular passage of Scripture speak to you? How did it help you?

15. What sometimes keeps you from praying? Why?

16. In Philippians 4:13, Paul said, "I can do everything through Him who gives me strength." If you said this, what specific things would you be doing?

17. Read Matthew 11:28-30. Name the actions we are to take. What action will Jesus take? You have already written your major stress-producer on your Post-it note. Write a plan of action for reducing this stress. Think about specific ways you can come to Jesus, take His yoke, and learn from Him. Keep this note in a prominent place (at your favorite Scripture, in your purse—wherever your eye often stops) to remind you this week of how to lighten your burden.

18. Pray that each woman present might experience some degree of relief in her specific stress. Thank Jesus for His promise of rest for our inner beings.

IT'S ABOUT TIME
De-Stress by
Setting Priorities

Matthew 6:25-34

OBJECTIVE
Evaluate priorities and schedule time for them.

LEADER PREPARATION
☙ Complete all activities in chapter 2.
☙ Bring squares of red, yellow, and green paper for each member. (Construction paper cut into squares about the size of an index card.)
☙ Adjust the number of questions to the design of your group.

GROUP TIME
1. Pray that each woman will be able to set aside her busy day and focus on God's teaching.
2 Each member should have a red, yellow, and green square representing colors in a traffic light. The leader should ask questions dealing with the last time they did a certain activity while the group responds with the appropriate color.

☙ Green = Within the last week. (Going great.)
☙ Yellow = Within the last month. (Caution, on brink of being neglected.)
☙ Red = So long ago I can't remember. (Danger, activity has stopped.)

The leader may create questions or choose from the following: When was the last time . . .

(a) you had a date with your husband? (Just the two of you.)
(b) you washed the windows?
(c) you exercised?
(d) your family did something as a unit? (No friends.)
(e) you cooked a meal?
(f) you kissed your husband?
(g) you talked to your best friend?
(h) you had a "quiet time" with God?
(i) you wrote a letter?
(j) you did laundry?
(k) you hugged your child?
(l) you did something nice for yourself?

3. Read Matthew 6:25-34. What principles in the passage would help us live better?
4. According to this passage, why will God take care of our needs? What other reasons can you think of?
5. What advice does Matthew 6:27 give about worrying? When is worrying good and when is it bad? Why do we worry?
6. Look more carefully at Matthew 6:33. What does seeking His kingdom and His righteousness mean?
7. What obstacles keep you from seeking God first?
8. Read Galatians 5:22. Which spiritual quality do you want to increase in your life? Why?
9. How could seeking God as your first priority reduce stress? How might seeking God as your first priority *increase* your stress?
10. What would you make time to do if you had a limited time to live?
11. What things keep you from pursuing your personal goals?
12. What was your favorite activity in this week's *From Stress to Action*? What did you learn from it? (Option: Divide into pairs for this question if time is short.)
13. Refer to the personal hourly schedule you created in your *Spiritual Notebook* and ideas gathered throughout your study of this chapter. Brainstorm ways to help each other save time.
14. Pray that God will provide new ways of making time for priorities this week. Ask Him to show you His kingdom and righteousness in a fresh way.

PROBLEMS TO PLUSES
De-Stress by
Gaining Perspective

Romans 5:1-5

OBJECTIVE
To begin to change our perspective of problems so we can look at long-term benefits.

LEADER PREPARATION
❧ Complete all activities in chapter 3.
❧ Think of an example of someone who has turned a problem into a benefit.
❧ Be prepared to share your cause-and-effect web from *From Stress to Action*, question 2.
❧ Adjust the number of questions to the design of your group.

GROUP TIME
1. Open with sentence prayers: "Thank You, God, for . . ."
2. Think of people who have turned a problem into a plus. Describe the process the person might have undergone. Examples: Joni Eareckson Tada, Helen Keller, or a friend of yours.
3. Read Romans 5:1-5 aloud. According to these verses, what does God give us?
4. What does each step mean to you?
5. In Romans 5:1-5, what does gaining access to God by faith in Jesus Christ mean?
6. Explain the meaning of Romans 5:1-5 by referring to the diagram on page 26.
7. When do you feel closer to God? When circumstances are good? or when you are having problems? Explain.

8. Can you have peace with God without *feeling* His peace? How?
9. How did Joseph's life illustrate Romans 5:1-5? (Summarize the chart on pages 26–27.
10. If someone has wronged you, how would having the perspective of Joseph help you forgive that person?
11. How does Romans 5:1-5 fit into your life? What stage are you currently experiencing and how can you see this stage moving into another stage?
12. In view of Romans 5:3-5, how can coping with a problem for a long period of time help you?
13. Which part of Romans 5:1-5 is the easiest to practice? Which is the most difficult?
14. Do you think a person must experience pain and problems to develop a strong character? Why or why not?
15. What points from the narrative section helped you?
16. Refer to activity 2 in *From Stess to Action* along with your *Spiritual Notebook*. What did you learn by doing the cause-and-effect web? (Option: discuss by dividing into pairs.)
17. What lessons could be learned from these trials: financial problems, having a handicapped child, having a problem teenager, health problems, a difficult marriage, having an impossible boss or coworker, unemployment. (Option: continue discussion by pairs. Address as many topics as time allows.)
18. Are you handling your stress differently than you did prior to beginning this study? Which ideas are making a difference in your life?
19. Pray together that God will help you see problems with His perspective.

Group Study 4

THE FACT IS...
De-Stress by
Using the Will

Psalm 22

OBJECTIVE

To draw on facts as well as feelings when we respond to circumstances.

LEADER PREPARATION

❧ Complete all activities in chapter 4.

❧ Be prepared to share how knowing God better has helped your faith.

❧ Adjust the number of questions to the design of your group.

GROUP TIME

1. Open with sentence prayers, stating a fact about God. "God, You are . . ."

2. Divide the group into pairs. Brainstorm for five minutes and then act out one of the situations in activity 1, of *From Stress to Action* on pages 43–44. (Refer also to your *Spiritual Notebook.*) One person will act out the feeling side and the other will act out the fact side. Evaluate under which circumstances one or the other might be most helpful.

3. Skim Psalm 22. Look back at the chart on page 36 and read each group of verses out loud. Explain what fact or feeling is shown in each.

4. David's psalms typically end on a positive note. Why?

5. Should you express your true feelings to God? Why or why not?

6. When is it helpful and when is it harmful to express your feelings to another person?

7. How could the facts you found about God in question 9 of *From Stress to Source,* help you when your feelings are taking over your thoughts?
8. What could you do on a regular basis to find more facts about God?
9. Describe the power of choice and how it effects your behavior.
10. Does making decisions increase or decrease your stress? Why?
11. How might responding to your family by facts instead of feelings provide a calmer atmosphere in your home?
12. What points stood out to you from the narrative section, *From Stress to Strength?*
13. What triggers you into an inappropriate emotional response? What steps could you take to control this in the future?
14. Continue to practice what you have already learned in the study. Share a success (or failure) story.
15. Close in prayer. Ask God to show you new reasons, based on His capabilities, to trust Him.

Group Study 5

WHO, ME?
De-Stress by Loving

1 Corinthians 13

OBJECTIVE
To begin to practice God's unconditional love toward others.

LEADER PREPARATION
❧ Complete all activities in chapter 5.
❧ Bring a 3-D poster (optional).
❧ Bring a large chart or board and notebook paper.
❧ Adjust the number of questions to the design of your group.

GROUP TIME
1. Before or after the meeting, have fun looking at the 3-D poster.
2. Open with sentence prayers: "Lord, I love You because . . ."
3. On a chart, list the roles or jobs women play in their daily lives (wife, rancher, teacher, mother, executive, other). Across from each job, list a few words to show top qualities for that position. For example:

Role or Job	Quality
Teacher	Patient; able to improve children's learning skills.
Cook	Able to plan creative, nutritious menus.

Each person should choose a different job and write a sentence, using the language from 1 Corinthians 13:1-3. For example, "If I am patient with my students every day and teach all children to read three grade levels above their age, but have not love, I have accomplished nothing." Read the sentences out loud. (Collect them; type into one paragraph; make copies for each member and distribute at the next meeting. Each woman will then have a modern "Love Chapter.")

4. Read 1 Corinthians 13. What truths did you find in this chapter?

5. In verses 1-3, why do you think God doesn't honor spiritual gifts if the person doesn't also have love?

6. Describe love by using verses 4-7.

7. How does stress interfere with practicing these qualities?

8. Refer to question 8, in *From Stress to Source.* How did Christ's life show perfect love in these Scriptures?

9. What does Jesus tell us to do about people who are hard to love? (See Matthew 5:43-48.)

10. Would following this example lead to more stress or less stress in your life? Why?

11. Why did Jesus want us to love in the same way that He loved? (See John 13:34.)

12. 1 Corinthians 13:12 promises a new understanding of things we can't know on earth. What things do you hope to see more clearly when that time comes?

13. What's the difference between loving someone and liking that person? Which do you think God is commanding us to do?

14. How could you apply 1 Corinthians 13:4-7? Refer to answers in your *Spiritual Notebook* for activity 1 of *From Stress to Action.* Share as many as time allows.

15. What effect did memorizing and saying 1 Corinthians 13:4-7 three times a day have on your life this week? Refer to *From Stress to Action,* activity 2. If you didn't do this activity, try it in the coming week.

16. Pray that each of you can practice Christ's kind of love in the coming week.

NOBODY'S PERFECT
De-Stress by
Releasing Perfectionism

Philippians 3:1-16

OBJECTIVE
To learn the difference between pursuing high standards and being obsessed with perfection.

LEADER PREPARATION
❧ Complete all activities in chapter 6.
❧ Bring paper and pencils.
❧ Adjust the number of questions to the design of your group.

GROUP TIME
1. Read Psalm 139:14. Pray asking God to reveal to each woman good qualities about herself. Take time for silent prayer, thanking God for how He made us.
2. Experiment with uncomfortable feelings, by drawing the best dinosaur you can in three minutes. Exchange papers with a partner. Tell each other what's good about the dinosaur and what could be improved. Thank the other person for giving constructive criticism.
3. How did you feel when the other person told you how your picture could be better? How could this demonstration with criticism apply to an area about which you really care?
4. Read Philippians 3:1-16. What did you learn from this passage?
5. How could following the guidelines in this passage help to de-stress your life?
6. What benefits would "rejoicing in the Lord" give you?
7. What requirements does Paul make for Christians in Philippians 3:3?

8. What traps of legalism do Christians fall into today? How can we prevent this?
9. What is the difference between keeping the law and having faith in Christ's righteousness? Which do you think is easier? Explain.
10. What practical steps can we take to know Christ?
11. Look more carefully at verses 12-16. What is Paul's technique for "pressing on"? Does this work for you?
12. In what areas do high standards cross the line into over-perfectionism?
13. How do you feel when you are around someone who seems overly perfect?
14. When an unexpected visitor catches you and your house in a mess, how do you handle it?
15. Most people feel better about themselves when they do good things. How can we keep our self-worth from being dependent on our works?
16. Explain Romans 3:21-28 as if you're talking to a child. (Refer to your answer for question 2, *From Stress to Action* in your *Spiritual Notebook.*)
17. What new insights did God reveal to you about perfectionism this week?
18. What did you appreciate in the narrative section, *From Stress to Strength?*
19. As you try to practice the teachings addressed during the last few weeks, what changes can you see in yourself?
20. Pray. Ask God to help you with the process of becoming all He has in mind for us to become.

A NEW WORD—NO!
De-Stress by Setting Limits

Exodus 18

OBJECTIVE

To set limits on our own activities so we can focus on God's agenda.

TEACHER PREPARATION

❦ Complete all activities in chapter 7.

❦ Be prepared to share a specific time when you believe that God directed your actions.

❦ Adjust the number of questions to the design of your group.

GROUP TIME

1. Read Ephesians 2:10. Pray with this verse in mind.
2. Brainstorm various ways to politely say "no."
3. Allow time to skim Exodus 18. What lessons did Moses learn?
4. How could these lessons help you?
5. If you were Zipporah, what would you say about your life with Moses?
6. Using verses 1-12, describe Jethro, Moses' father-in-law.
7. What does this chapter reveal about the relationship between Moses and Jethro?
8. Why do you think Moses didn't recognize that he had an administration problem before Jethro pointed it out?
9. Why did Moses feel so responsible for the people? (verses 15-16)
10. Do you think that Moses was "playing God"? Why or why not?
11. According to verses 19-23, what solution did Jethro give Moses?
12. How can we assume too much responsibility at home? At work? At church?

13. Do you like feeling indispensable? Why or why not?
14. When and why is it difficult for you to ask someone for help?
15. What benefits can result from sharing responsibilities?
16. How are other people affected when you get bogged down with responsibility?
17. In view of verses 24-26, what type of person do you think Moses chose to help him?
18. What are some vital reasons for saying "no"? For saying "yes"?
19. How did God direct your actions after practicing *From Stress to Action*, activity 4?
20. Close with silent prayer, focusing on ways God might use us.

Group Study 8

KEEPING FIT
De-Stress by
Practicing Good Habits

1 Thessalonians 5:12-24

OBJECTIVE
To form good habits that keep you physically, intellectually, emotionally, and spiritually fit.

LEADER PREPARATION
❧ Complete all activities in chapter 8.
❧ Pray for each woman in her commitment to form good habits.
❧ Be prepared to share your successes and failures in staying fit.
❧ Bring small squares of paper, pencils, and a basket.
❧ Adjust the number of questions to the design of your group.

GROUP TIME
1. Read Matthew 22:37-39. Pray with these verses in mind.
2. Pass out several squares of paper to each person. Ask the group to write down actions that make them feel better (one on each square). Put the papers into a basket and draw them out one at a time. The group should classify each action into the areas of physical, intellectual, emotional, or spiritual.
3. Refer to *From Stress to Action*, activity 2, in your *Spiritual Notebook*. Which action under each area did you think was the best for you to do? How did it work this week? Will you continue next week?
4. Read 1 Thessalonians 5:12-24. Summarize what Paul is teaching us in this passage.
5. Review 1 Thessalonians 5:12-15. Which instructions would be hardest for you to follow? Why?

6. Who are your spiritual leaders? (Not just your pastor.)
7. What would you do if you disagreed with these leaders on a spiritual issue?
8. How can you practice 1 Thessalonians 5:12-15 at church? At home? At work?
9. What does Paul say to do for yourself in 1 Thessalonians 5:16-18?
10. How can practicing this help manage stress?
11. How can a busy person pray continually throughout the day?
12. How can you thank God even in difficult circumstances?
13. Do you think that Paul is telling us to deny reality by practicing verses 16-18? Why or why not?
14. How might the instructions of 1 Thessalonians 5:19-22 lead toward spiritual fitness?
15. How can we stifle the Holy Spirit?
16. How can you test new teaching?
17. What personal encouragement do you find in 1 Thessalonians 5:23-24?
18. What will help you to keep practicing Paul's advice in this entire passage?
19. Have you changed any actions or attitudes as a result of this book? If so, what?
20. Pray sentence prayers: "Lord, help me to . . ."

THE TAPESTRY COLLECTION

Michelle Booth, *Gold in the Ashes*
Eight Studies on Wisdom from Job

Michelle Booth, *Steadfast Faith in Times of Turmoil*
Eight Studies to Toughen Your Faith

Karen Dockrey, *Tuned-Up Parenting*
Eight Studies to Invite Harmony into Your Home

Marion Duckworth, *Pure Passion*
Eight Studies on The Song of Solomon

Marion Duckworth, *Renewed on the Run*
Nine Studies on 1 Peter for Women on the Move

Lin Johnson, *Prayer Patterns*
Ten Prayers to Weave the Fabric of Your Life

Vicki Lake, *Restored in the Ruins*
Eight Studies on Nehemiah

Ellen E. Larson and David V. Esterline, *More than a Story*
Nine Studies on the Parables of Jesus

RuthAnn Ridley, *Every Marriage Is Different*
Eight Studies on Key Biblical Marriages

Beth Donigan Seversen, *Mirror Image*
Eight Studies from Colossians

Diane Stout, *De-Stressing Your Life*
Eight Studies to Cushion Life's Pressures